Almost everybody has jumped on the AI train now, but nobody knows where they're heading. The train is moving so fast that they can't see the scenery out the window.

New technology is always good. I had no choice but to take this train. I don't want to return to the Stone Age without AI.

I think AI is good, but I feel dizzy because it's moving too quickly. Can anyone help me?

I'm so happy that I got on this train finally! I'm sure my future will be bright.

Oh, please let me get off right now! I didn't know it was going to be so fast. I'm afraid this train might derail at any moment!

I've tried to dissuade people from getting on the AI train. I warned them that nobody knows the final destination. Even if they are able to reach the destination, it may be a place they never imagined. I'm sure they will face an appalling reality when the train finally stops.

— It's been raining heavily for weeks. Do you know why?
— How can I know why exactly? But I guess it's because of CLIMATE CHANGE. Recently, we have alternated between severe drought and flooding.
— I disagree. I think God is outraged, and he's decided to destroy the earth with a great flood.
— What should we do?
— Haven't you read the Bible?
— Not yet.
— God ordered Noah to make an ark for the coming flood. We have to make a boat too and stock it with food.
— What should we prepare?
— Some Big Macs and our smartphones. We could survive for some time on Big Macs, and we'll need our smartphones to see the weather forecast.

— Let me show you our two labs: this is the vaccine development lab, and that is the virus development lab.
— What? I don't understand why you need a lab for virus development.
— It's as simple as that. If we don't have new viruses, we won't be able to develop proper vaccines. We have already developed thousands of new viruses!
— What if some of them escape "by mistake"? I'm scared of what would happen!
— You don't have to worry about a thing. We have all kinds of vaccines for currently developed viruses. We're ready to sell our vaccines at any time.

It's so easy to escape from this lab! It seems that researchers aren't strictly controlling us ON PURPOSE. We'll spread like wildfire and prey on people before the vaccine is available. In particular, kids and elderly people will be easy prey for us!

Dog: I'm very disappointed with my dad. They're definitely child slaves! He's turning a blind eye to social injustice. I'm going to run after them until I rescue them. God help me!

What are you talking about? Don't you know slavery was abolished 160 years ago? That can't be human trafficking. I think they're going to school.

Dad, take a look at them! They look scared and need our help. They look like slaves! Something must be done immediately!

OPEN TO DEBATE 2

Major New Edition

30 GLOBAL ISSUES

WRITTEN BY LIS KOREA EDITORIAL STAFF & NEAL D. WILLIAMS

Introduction

    This discussion book has been written for English language students who wish to study contemporary global topics in English. The book considers a wide range of issues, from *euthanasia* to *terrorism*, from *gender equality* to *Internet addiction*, from *COVID* to *LGBTQ*. Each unit is introduced with a topic preview, consisting of several thought-provoking questions. The preview is followed by an authentic model conversation in which two individuals discuss an aspect of the issue being considered in the unit. These conversations use idiomatic language, the same type of language that native speakers of English use in normal dialogue. Next, there is a reading passage that provides an overview of the main ideas related to the issue. Every attempt has been made to use the most current information, statistics, and perspectives in the reading section. Key words and expressions are highlighted in the reading passage.

    Following the reading passage, the key words and expressions are defined in easy-to-understand language. Each key word or expression is then used in a sentence in order to illustrate the meaning in context. As every student of the English language knows, an individual word can have numerous meanings, and common words can have uncommon meanings. Therefore, each word or expression that is defined in this book is given the proper definition that fits with the context of the reading passage. For example, the most common meaning of the word *weight* is "a measurement that indicates how heavy a person or thing is." However, *weight* can also refer to "a type of burden or stress." The latter definition is the only one that applies to the reading passage in this book, so that is the only definition that is cited.

    After key words and expressions are defined, readers are given seven questions designed to provoke discussion. These questions are almost all questions of opinion, not questions of fact. In other words, students should feel free to express their own opinion since there is no right or wrong answer to the questions. Some of the questions are simply fascinating quotes that can be used as a basis for discussion.

    Finally, as an added bonus, each unit concludes with a "current hot topic." There is a short reading passage about a controversial aspect of the topic being considered in the unit, along with two discussion questions.

Dedication
This book is dedicated to my lovely wife and best friend, *Eunkyung Won*.

Suggestions to the Student

Carnegie Hall in New York City was opened in 1891 and is now one of the world's most famous concert halls. Every musician dreams of performing there at some point in their career. An old joke asks the question: "How do you get to Carnegie Hall?" The answer: "Practice, practice, practice!" Many students of the English language frequently ask their teacher a similar question: "How can I become a great English speaker?" The best answer is: "Speak, speak, speak!" Of course, you have to know some grammar and vocabulary, but once you have a reasonable knowledge of those aspects, your skill in speaking English will depend on how much time you spend actually using the language.

Studies have shown that English speakers can become fairly fluent in Spanish with about 600 hours of practice. The same is true of Spanish speakers who want to learn English. The amount of time needed is fairly low because English and Spanish are somewhat similar. However, if an English speaker wants to learn Korean, that learner will need to invest about 2,200 hours of practice in using the language, and the same is true for a Korean speaker who wants to learn English. The two languages are dramatically different in appearance, grammar, and pronunciation, so much more time is needed. If you want to become a skillful English speaker, you need to accumulate as much time as possible in actually speaking the language.

One easy way to build up time in speaking English is to enroll in an English conversation class. When you are in your class, you should speak as much as you can. It is important that you do not worry about using the correct grammar; just keep speaking, and you will communicate. You will also, slowly but surely, improve your conversational skills. The English learners who have become fluent in English are no smarter than you. They just kept trying to use English and speaking as much as possible until they gained some level of fluency. You can do the same!

Suggestions to the Teacher

If you are an English language teacher, you are naturally interested in inspiring your students to speak English as much as possible. How can this goal be accomplished? Here are several practical suggestions. First, it is important to emphasize to students that the discussion questions written in this book simply provide an opportunity to express one's opinion. There is no right or wrong answer. Language experts say that one of the most important duties of a language teacher is to reduce anxiety in the classroom. Therefore, it is crucial to convince students that everyone's opinion is valid and important.

Second, because the aim of a language course is to get students involved in speaking the language as much as possible, it is better to use pair work than group discussions. When students are in groups, they may feel intimidated by more fluent speakers, and they will feel reluctant to speak. However, if they are working in pairs, they are conversing with a partner and have no choice but to speak. As they speak more with their partner, they will gain in confidence and fluency.

Third, teachers need to emphasize to students that simply *trying* to speak in English will help them achieve their goal of fluency. Of course, students will often experience some stress when trying to express their opinion in another language. They may feel as though their grammar and vocabulary are inadequate and that they should speak using only grammar that is completely accurate. Effective teachers will explain to students that it's necessary to feel some stress, but that's not anything to worry about. Students should just keep talking, using the vocabulary and grammar that they already know. Over time, they will improve in speaking, as well as in vocabulary and grammar.

Open to Debate (2): 30 Global Issues
Table of Contents

Introduction	06
Suggestions to the Student	07
Suggestions to the Teacher	08

Issue 01	Access to Education	10	Issue 16	Immigration ... 70
Issue 02	Artificial Intelligence	14	Issue 17	Internet Addiction ... 74
Issue 03	Child Labor and Trafficking	18	Issue 18	Internet Censorship ... 78
Issue 04	Child Marriage	22	Issue 19	LGBTQ ... 82
Issue 05	Climate Change	26	Issue 20	Life Expectancy ... 86
Issue 06	Corruption	30	Issue 21	Natural Disasters ... 90
Issue 07	COVID-19	34	Issue 22	Obesity ... 94
Issue 08	Digital Currencies	38	Issue 23	Pollution ... 98
Issue 09	Drug Abuse	42	Issue 24	Population Growth ... 102
Issue 10	Euthanasia	46	Issue 25	Same-Sex Marriage ... 106
Issue 11	Factory Farming	50	Issue 26	Smoking in Developing Countries ... 110
Issue 12	Gender Equality	54	Issue 27	Social Media ... 114
Issue 13	Great Power Conflicts	58	Issue 28	Suicide ... 118
Issue 14	Human Trafficking	62	Issue 29	Surveillance and Privacy ... 122
Issue 15	Hunger and Malnourishment	66	Issue 30	Terrorism ... 126

Appendix: Notes about Grammar and Style	128
Discussion Textbooks from LIS KOREA	130

I'm 80 years YOUNG, and I still like to LEARN SOMETHING.

I'm 15 years OLD, but I like to LEARN NOTHING.

I'm lucky that I learned how to stay young as soon as I was born. Mom, please buy me all the books in the world. I want to start learning in this cradle.

Topic Preview:

Does everyone in your country have access to a good education? How many years of education are legally required in your country? Must every student graduate from high school? Can anyone go to college? Who pays for college fees?

Dialogue:

Jack: Nora, may I ask you a personal question?

Nora: Sure, if it's not too personal.

Jack: I was just wondering if you are involved in any charities.

Nora: Yes, I am, actually. I support Save the Children.

Jack: Oh, I've heard of them. They do good work.

Nora: Yes, they do. In my case, I sponsor a young girl in Zambia.

Jack: Wow! That's impressive. How do you support her?

Nora: I make a monthly donation that helps provide her with access to good nutrition, health, and education.

Jack: That's wonderful! Can you show me how to sponsor a child?

Nora: Of course! I'll send you a link to the website.

Access to Education

An 11-year-old girl named Nafissa dreams of becoming a nurse. Unfortunately, she lives in the country of Niger, where the average girl stays in school for only five years. Due to Nafissa's lack of educational opportunities, she may never be able to fulfill her dream. She is one of millions of children who do not have access to a proper education.

One of the important slogans of UNICEF states, "Every child has the right to learn." In the modern world, one would think that every nation should be able to provide a basic education to each of its children. Sadly, many countries still suffer from a lack of trained teachers, insufficient learning materials, and poor sanitation. In addition, many children come to school too hungry, sick, or exhausted from work to gain much benefit from their education. This sad situation was only worsened by the COVID-19 pandemic, which began in 2020 and whose effects continue to this day. In fact, more than 600 million children and adolescents around the world are unable to reach minimum proficiency levels in reading, writing, and mathematics.

In order to remedy the current dire situation in global education, the United Nations has established some key goals that must be accomplished by the year 2030. Above all, the international community must ensure that all girls and boys have access to quality early childhood development and preprimary education. That must be followed up with free, equitable, and quality primary education and secondary education. Also, the world's leaders must ensure equal access for all women and men to an affordable vocational and university education. By 2030, we must eliminate gender disparities in education and ensure equal access to all levels of education. Finally, we must dramatically increase the supply of qualified teachers through international cooperation in teacher training.

ISSUE 01 ACCESS TO EDUCATION

Vocabulary & Expressions:

UNICEF
*an organization originally known as the "United Nations International Children's Emergency Fund," but now usually known simply as the "United Nations Children's Fund"
- *UNICEF* was awarded the Nobel Peace Prize in 1965 for their work in providing humanitarian aid to children worldwide.

sanitation
*the process of keeping things free from filth, infection, or other dangers to health
- Almost every city has a department of *sanitation* that is responsible for collecting and disposing of garbage as well as sweeping the streets.

pandemic
*an outbreak of a disease that occurs over a wide geographic area, often including multiple countries and continents
- An *epidemic* is an outbreak of disease that spreads quickly and affects many people; a *pandemic* is an epidemic that spreads over a wide geographic area.

proficiency
*having skill or competence in any art, science, or subject
- All high school graduates should have *proficiency* in basic mathematics.

remedy
*to provide a cure or solution for a problem; to relieve
- The government can *remedy* the problem of poverty by guaranteeing every citizen a minimum monthly income.

dire
*very urgent or serious
- The many homeless people in our city are in *dire* need of help in getting food and health care.

preprimary education
*a period of education where children learn simple skills, such as writing the alphabet, reading simple words, counting, and following basic directions
- The period of *preprimary education* usually includes kindergarten.

equitable
*showing fairness and treating everyone equally
- In an equitable system of *education*, girls and boys have the same level of access to education.

primary education
*when children learn basic subjects, such as reading, writing, math, science, and social studies
- The period of *primary education* usually includes elementary school and middle school.

secondary education
*a period of schooling between middle school and college, where students study advanced math, English, science, and history
- The period of *secondary education* is usually the same as high school.

gender disparity
*an unfair difference between the opportunities for men and women; also known as *gender inequality*
- Most countries have eliminated *gender disparities* in elementary education, but inequalities in secondary education and beyond are still widespread.

Open to Debate (2): 30 Global Issues

Discussion Points:

1. Do you know anyone who has traveled to Africa to help local people? What was their experience like?
2. Who do you think should be responsible for improving access to education around the world?
3. How did the COVID-19 pandemic affect education in your country? How were you affected?
4. In your country, what percentage of young people go to college? Who pays for college?
5. How is primary and secondary education funded in your country? Is it free for everyone?

Read the following quotes about education.
Can you explain what they mean? Do you agree with the idea expressed?

6. Education is, quite simply, peace-building by another name. It is the most effective form of defense spending there is.
   Kofi Annan, Former United Nations Secretary-General
7. If you educate a man, you educate an individual, but if you educate a woman, you educate a nation. African proverb

Current Hot Topic: Learning Poverty

The term "learning poverty" refers to a tragic, contemporary situation: more than half of children in low- and middle-income countries cannot read and understand a simple story by age 10. In poor countries, the level is as high as 80%. The World Bank has launched a new program to cut the learning poverty rate by at least half before the year 2030. To accomplish this aim, the World Bank and UNESCO will help countries improve their learning systems and ensure better learning conditions, including better water and sanitation and improved health and nutrition.

For Further Discussion:

1. Do you think the World Bank can meet its goal to cut the learning poverty rate in half by 2030? Would you be willing for your country to donate more money toward this goal?
2. How would you describe the learning environment for children in your country? How could it be improved?

Almost everybody has jumped on the AI train now, but nobody knows where they're heading. The train is moving so fast that they can't see the scenery out the window.

New technology is always good. I had no choice but to take this train. I don't want to return to the Stone Age without AI.

I think AI is good, but I feel dizzy because it's moving too quickly. Can anyone help me?

I'm so happy that I got on this train finally! I'm sure my future will be bright.

Oh, please let me get off right now! I didn't know it was going to be so fast. I'm afraid this train might derail at any moment!

I've tried to dissuade people from getting on the AI train. I warned them that nobody knows the final destination. Even if they are able to reach the destination, it may be a place they never imagined. I'm sure they will face an appalling reality when the train finally stops.

Topic Preview:

What do you think is the future of artificial intelligence (AI)? Will it be helpful or harmful to mankind? In what ways do you use AI nowadays? How do you expect to use it in the future?

Dialogue:

Grace: Henry, I hear that you're pretty good with computer technology.

Henry: I don't want to brag, but I think I'm pretty proficient. Do you have a computer problem?

Grace: Not really, but I do need some help. I'm trying to locate a friend from high school that I've lost touch with.

Henry: I see. And you want to find this person using the Internet.

Grace: Yes, that's right. Do you know of any way to search for a person? I have several photographs of her.

Henry: Well, you should go to PimEyes.com. They use facial recognition software to search billions of web pages for a particular person.

Grace: Wow! I had no idea there was a site that could do that. Does it cost anything?

Henry: Well, you'll have to buy a membership for one month, which is $30.

Grace: That's not too bad. Okay. Can you show me how to do it?

Henry: Sure. Let's just sit down at my computer, and I'll show you how it works.

Grace: Thanks. I had no idea that AI had advanced so far!

Artificial Intelligence

In March 2016, the Republic of Korea was on edge. It seemed as though the weight of the nation rested on one man's shoulders. A Korean man named Lee Sedol was competing against a computer program named AlphaGo for a $1 million prize. The goal: to see who could win a five-game match of *baduk*, which is also known as *go*. In the end, the computer won four games out of five. However, Lee won the fourth game with his brilliant play and because he, as a human, could do one thing that AlphaGo could not: he could adjust his play based on what he saw his opponent do in previous games.

While human-computer competitions like the one in Korea may be entertaining, they raise some important questions for all of humanity. How can we harness the power of artificial intelligence (AI) to benefit human beings in practical ways, and how do we ensure that AI does not become so powerful that it harms us? The advantages of AI are obvious: machines can make accurate decisions with zero human error, they can make decisions much faster than humans, they work endlessly and don't get tired, and they have no emotions to get in the way of decision-making. The disadvantages of AI are also clear: AI machines are very expensive to produce, they lack creativity, they take away jobs from humans, they do not understand ethics, and with their lack of emotions, they do a poor job at customer service.

On the positive side, AI is being used nowadays to produce better diagnoses of cancer. On the negative side, it can sometimes create mayhem, as happened at a high-tech fair in Shenzhen, where a robot attacked a display booth and injured a young boy. With AI, we must proceed with caution.

ISSUE 02 ARTIFICIAL INTELLIGENCE

Vocabulary & Expressions:

on edge
*being anxious or nervous
- The family was *on edge* as they waited for the results of the medical tests.

weight
*a mental or moral burden; the stress of a responsibility
- My mother had to bear the *weight* of taking care of my sick grandmother for many years.

to rest on one's shoulders
*to have the responsibility or blame for a certain task
- For most young people, the burden of paying for their college education *rests on their parents' shoulders*.

AlphaGo
*a computer program, developed by Google, that plays the board game *baduk*, also known as *go*
- In October 2015, in a match against Fan Hui, *AlphaGo* became the first computer program to defeat a human professional *baduk* player.

brilliant
*very intelligent or clever
- Warren Buffet is recognized around the world as a *brilliant* investor.

base on
*to create or develop an action, plan, conclusion, or opinion on the basis of something else
- The award-winning film *The King's Speech* (2010) is *based on* a true story.

harness
*to utilize or put to work
- Sunlight can be *harnessed* to create electricity.

to get in the way of
*to hinder, obstruct, or prevent something from happening
- Students must not let personal hobbies *get in the way of* their education.

ethics
*rules of good behavior based on what is morally good and bad
- Most business schools require students to take a course in business *ethics*.

diagnosis
*the act of identifying a disease from its signs and symptoms; plural = *diagnoses*
- Before a doctor can treat your illness, she must first make a proper *diagnosis*.

mayhem
*actions that hurt people and destroy things; a situation that involves a lot of violence
- In the 1984 film *The Terminator*, the main character (Arnold Schwarzenegger) creates a lot of *mayhem* before he is eliminated.

Open to Debate (2): **30 Global Issues**

Discussion Points:

1. Can you cite some examples of how AI has benefited people?
2. Can you cite some examples of how AI has harmed people?
3. How are companies in your country developing AI? Would you like to work for one of them?
4. Do law enforcement agencies in your country use facial recognition systems? Do you think this technology is safe and valuable?
5. Do you, or someone you know, use any "virtual assistants," such as Amazon Alexa, Google Assistant, Siri, or Bixby? How are they useful?
6. What are your favorite movies featuring AI (e.g., *The Matrix*, *The Terminator*, *Robocop*)?
7. Elon Musk, the CEO of Tesla, has said, "AI is far more dangerous than nuclear weapons." Do you agree with his idea?

Current Hot Topic: Self-Driving Cars

Recently, two men were killed after their car, a Tesla 2019 Model S, crashed and caught fire near Houston, Texas. Witnesses said that the car was speeding when it suddenly went off the road and hit a tree. Police investigators believe that neither man was actually driving the car. Apparently, they were using the Tesla's autopilot, which is a self-driving feature. According to Tesla, when a driver is using the autopilot feature, they must still pay attention to driving. However, some Tesla drivers have failed to understand that message. We must ask: are the highways truly ready for self-driving cars?

For Further Discussion:

1. Have you heard about any self-driving cars in your country? What company is making them?
2. Would you be willing to take a nap in a self-driving car while it's driving?

— Do you have kids working here?
— Yes, we do. Is there a problem, officer?
— Don't you know that child labor is illegal?
— I know, but finding the right job is very important for their future.
— I don't understand what you mean.
— It's hard to explain. Why don't you just take a look at what they're doing?

Our job is learning and playing. These activities will be our stepping stones for a bright future.

That's right. I want be the next Michael Jordan!

I'm a wannabe pop star! I have to practice playing the guitar day and night.

Topic Preview:

What do you know about child labor and trafficking? Does it ever occur in your country? Is it legal for children to work in your country? Can children work in a family business? Is it possible that you own some products that were made by child labor (e.g., shoes, clothing, coffee)?

Dialogue:

Mia: Hey, Lucas. Where are you going with that soccer ball?

Lucas: I'm going out to play soccer with my friends. Want to join us?

Mia: Oh, sorry. I have to study for a test.

Lucas: Well, maybe next time.

Mia: By the way, where did you buy that soccer ball?

Lucas: I bought it at the sporting goods store downtown. Why do you ask?

Mia: Well, I just hope it's not one of those balls made by child labor.

Lucas: I don't think so. It's an Adidas brand. I don't think a famous company like that would use child labor.

Mia: Well, I hope you're right. I just remember a few years ago when there was a huge scandal about soccer balls being made with child labor.

Lucas: Hmmm… well, I will write the company and see what they say about that.

Child Labor and Trafficking

Gita is only 12 years old, but she already performs more labor than many adults. She works from 4:00 am to 10:00 pm every day in a carpet factory in Nepal, with only one hour's break in the afternoon. She says, "My fingers hurt from knotting the threads, my eyes hurt from looking at the design map, and I sit down for hours, so it really hurts my legs." In Nepal, the minimum wage is about $4.50 per day, but the majority of child laborers make far less. Like Gita, millions of children in other countries face a life of misery.

The number of children forced into child labor has risen to 160 million worldwide. After 2000, the use of child labor was on a downward trend, but the advent of the COVID-19 pandemic made matters worse. In poor countries, more than 20% of children are involved in labor, according to UNICEF. In addition, 30 million children live outside their country of birth, increasing their risk of being trafficked for sexual exploitation and other work. It would be a mistake to think that child labor is only present in poor countries. Human Rights Watch has reported extensively on the dangers that children face while working in various agricultural jobs in the United States. Under US law, children as young as 12 can work unlimited hours on farms if they have parental permission, as long as they don't miss school. This policy is clearly out of step with international labor standards.

In 1990, the United Nations adopted the Convention on the Rights of the Child, which established legal rules for protecting children from labor. If the principles of this treaty were followed, child labor would be completely eliminated. This document has been ratified by every nation, except the United States.

ISSUE 03 CHILD LABOR AND TRAFFICKING

Vocabulary & Expressions:

perform *to carry out, do
- Every job has specific tasks that a worker must **perform**.

knot the threads *to tie textile fibers into a certain arrangement
- To **knot the threads** properly is a difficult but important step in knitting and sewing.

minimum wage *the lowest amount that an employer can legally pay a worker
- Many American workers want the **minimum wage** to be raised to $15 per hour.

downward trend *a general tendency or direction that is moving to a lower condition
- The stock market is on a **downward trend**, so it's not a good time to invest in stocks.

advent *the arrival or coming of something
- When flowers begin to bloom, we know it's the **advent** of spring.

matters *the situation or subject that is being discussed or considered
- Mary was angry because her boyfriend was talking to another girl; however, he made **matters** worse by lying about the situation.

traffic *to buy or sell something, especially illegally; past tense = **trafficked**
- Criminal networks have **trafficked** in drugs and people for years.

exploitation *the action of treating someone unfairly in order to benefit from their work
- The CEO was arrested for the **exploitation** of foreign workers.

out of step with *not in harmony with others in a certain group
- The political candidate received only 10% of the vote, showing that he was **out of step with** most citizens.

adopt *to formally accept and put into action
- New York was the first state to **adopt** a law requiring drivers to wear seat belts.

ratify *to make a treaty or agreement official by signing it or voting for it
- Canada **ratified** the Convention on the Rights of the Child in 1991.

Open to Debate (2): 30 Global Issues

Discussion Points:

1. What is the minimum age for working in your country? Should it be increased?
2. Have you heard of any cases of child labor in your country? What happened?
3. How old were you when you had your first job? What kind of work did you do?
4. Is it common for high school students in your country to have a part-time job?
5. How would you respond if you found out that something you own, such as your smartphone or soccer ball, was produced by child labor?
6. Many Korean business owners have their children work in the family business. Do you think this case of child labor is acceptable?
7. If a business owner is caught using child labor, what punishment should they receive?

Current Hot Topic: US Failure to Ratify the Convention on the Rights of the Child

The Convention on the Rights of the Child was adopted by the United Nations General Assembly in 1989 and became effective the next year. It is shocking to realize that the US is the only country that has not ratified this treaty. The opposition to ratifying the treaty comes mainly from religious groups. They claim that the Convention conflicts with the US Constitution and that it could take away some rights of parents. They also claim that the US already has laws that protect the rights of children. Still, there is a movement of American citizens to ratify the treaty.

For Further Discussion:

1. Do you think the American objections to ratifying the Convention on the Rights of the Child are reasonable?
2. Would you agree with this statement: "The US cannot be a true leader for human rights until they ratify the Convention on the Rights of the Child"?

— I want some apples. How much are they?
— Two dollars for an apple.
— Who is she?
— She's my daughter, and she's on sale now.
— On sale? How much is she?
— Five thousand dollars.
— That's a bit expensive. Can I have a discount?
— No way! She is very cheap actually, I think, considering her age. She's just ten years old!
— Can I return her later if I don't like her?
— Yes, but I can't refund your money.

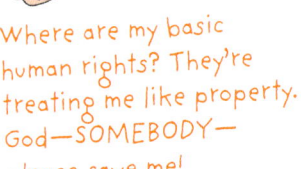

Where are my basic human rights? They're treating me like property. God—SOMEBODY—please save me!

Topic Preview:

How old should a person be before they are allowed to get married? Did any of your ancestors have to marry someone chosen by their parents? Would you like for your parents to choose your romantic partner? Should the United Nations require all countries to ban marriages of people younger than age 18?

Dialogue:

Mason: Sophia, I have a question for you. What is the minimum age for marriage in Canada?

Sophia: It's age 16 nationally, but each province can set a higher age if they want.

Mason: What about your province?

Sophia: Well, I'm from Manitoba, and the minimum age is 18 there.

Mason: I see. Well, that sounds reasonable.

Sophia: What about the US? Is there a national minimum age for marriage?

Mason: No, not on the federal level. Each state sets its own rules for marriage.

Sophia: There must be a lot of different rules since there are 50 states.

Mason: Yes, that's right. The minimum age ranges from 12 to 18, depending on which state you're in.

Sophia: Age 12? That sounds ridiculous!

Mason: I agree with you, but only one state has that law, and the couple must have their parents' permission. I think it never actually happens.

Child Marriage

A little girl named Gloria dreamed of getting an education. Unfortunately, she lived in rural Zambia, where many girls are forced into arranged marriages while they are very young. When Gloria's father died, her mother could not provide for herself and her 10 young children, so she arranged a marriage for Gloria with a 35-year-old man. Gloria's new husband was supposed to take care of Gloria's mother and siblings, but in the end, all he did was give a single goat to Gloria's family. In her new role as a wife, Gloria had to drop out of school and stay home to take care of her husband.

After six months of marriage, Gloria discovered that she was pregnant. While she was still pregnant, her husband died. After the funeral, her husband's brother inherited all his land and property, and he married Gloria as well. In this second marriage, Gloria was often subjected to domestic violence, and she suffered a miscarriage. Several years passed, and she got pregnant again. However, her second husband also died and Gloria, still a child herself, was left alone to give birth. Now her dream is that her son can get an education so that his life will be better than hers. Gloria says, "I would like to tell others that when you get married at an early age, things are difficult, you lose all your rights, and you suffer a lot."

Research on child marriage reveals that 40 million girls aged 15–19 are currently married or in a union worldwide. Each year about 12 million more girls will be forced into marriage before reaching age 18, and a third of those are under age 15. The United Nations has called for global action to end this hideous human rights violation by 2030.

ISSUE 04 CHILD MARRIAGE

Vocabulary & Expressions:

arranged marriage
*a marriage in which the husband and wife are chosen for each other by their parents
- About 75% of people in India prefer having an *arranged marriage*.

provide for
*to supply what is needed for something or someone
- Most parents feel a need to *provide for* their children's education.

drop out of
*to quit attending a school or training program
- Johnny Depp *dropped out of* high school at age 16 to become a rock musician.

inherit
*to receive money or property from someone when that person dies
- When Joe's grandmother died, he *inherited* $1 million from her.

subjected to
*exposed to or made vulnerable to some experience, often something negative
- New soldiers are *subjected to* strict rules of exercise and discipline.

domestic violence
*violence committed by one family member against another
- *Domestic violence* is often physical, but it can also be psychological.

miscarriage
*a condition in which a pregnancy ends too early and the baby does not survive
- Women older than age 35 have a higher risk of *miscarriage* than do younger women.

rights
*legal, social, or ethical privileges that one should have
- In a democracy, every citizen has the *rights* of voting, religion, and free speech.

union
*the situation where a couple lives together without being formally married
- In some countries, unmarried couples can live together in a civil *union* or partnership.

call for
*to make a request or demand for something
- The newspaper *called for* an investigation into the politician.

hideous
*morally offensive and shocking
- The *Silence of the Lambs* is a 1991 film about a serial killer's *hideous* crimes.

Open to Debate (2): 30 Global Issues

Discussion Points:

1. Were arranged marriages ever common in your country? Do they still happen today?
2. Why is child marriage wrong? What problems does it cause?
3. What do you think should be done to stop child marriages?
4. At what age can a person legally get married in your country?
5. Did your parents ever try to match you with a potential marriage partner? What happened?
6. What is the average age that young people get married in your country? Is the average age different for men and women?
7. In your opinion, what age is the best age to get married?

Current Hot Topic: Child Marriages in Developed Countries

It is wrong to think that child marriages only happen in poor, developing countries. Most people are shocked to learn that approximately 300,000 children under age 18 were married in the US between 2000 and 2018. In the US, there is no federal law regarding child marriage, so every state sets its own requirements. In more than 80% of the cases, child marriage involves a young girl and an older man. At present, child marriage is legal in most states. Human rights organizations like "Unchained at Last" are pressuring legislators to establish age 18 as a minimum age for marriage.

For Further Discussion:

1. Why do most cases of child marriage involve a young girl and an older man?
2. What do you think should be the minimum legal age for marriage? Should it be age 18, with no exceptions?

— It's been raining heavily for weeks. Do you know why?
— How can I know why exactly? But I guess it's because of CLIMATE CHANGE. Recently, we have alternated between severe drought and flooding.
— I disagree. I think God is outraged, and he's decided to destroy the earth with a great flood.
— What should we do?
— Haven't you read the Bible?
— Not yet.
— God ordered Noah to make an ark for the coming flood. We have to make a boat too and stock it with food.
— What should we prepare?
— Some Big Macs and our smartphones. We could survive for some time on Big Macs, and we'll need our smartphones to see the weather forecast.

● **Topic Preview:**

How concerned are you about climate change? How does climate change affect you personally? Are elementary and high school students required to study climate change in your country? Do you know anyone who denies that climate change is real?

● **Dialogue:**

Liam: Ava, I read that there are some politicians in the US who deny that climate change is real.

Ava: Yes, Liam, unfortunately that is true—sad but true.

Liam: How can they get elected to public office? I thought that everybody believed in climate change.

Ava: Well, there are a lot of conservative Republicans who think climate change is a hoax.

Liam: I find that hard to believe! About 97% of scientists say that global warming is real.

Ava: Yes, you're right, but there are some people who don't accept the science.

Liam: That's so sad. The US should be a leader in dealing with climate change.

Ava: I agree with you. However, about 70% of Americans believe that global warming is real.

Liam: Well, that's good to hear.

Ava: Yeah. At least there is some hope for the future.

Climate Change

For a while, Nausaleta Setani, a lady in her 50s, did not believe that climate change was real. However, she is now convinced of its reality, not just because of the science but because her daily life has become tougher due to the erratic movement of the sea. Setani lives in Tuvalu, which is the fourth smallest nation in the world and home to just 11,000 people. Tuvalu is composed of three reef islands and six atolls, which lie in the middle of the Pacific Ocean, about halfway between Hawaii and Australia.

In November 2021, Seve Paeniu, Tuvalu's finance minister, traveled to the United Nations Climate Change Conference in Glasgow, Scotland, to tell the world that his country is sinking beneath the waves and to plead for global action. Paeniu described his nation's plight in bleak terms: "We have land territory being submerged or disappearing where there used to be vegetation and agriculture. Food security has been severely harmed, and even our fisheries." To make matters worse, the number of devastating cyclones in the Pacific Ocean has increased. Former US President Barack Obama also sounded the alarm. He said, "Islands are the canary in the coal mine in this situation. They are sending a message now that if we don't act—and act boldly—it's going to be too late."

Earth's warming climate is the result of a buildup of greenhouse gases in the atmosphere, created primarily from the burning of fossil fuels for energy and other human activities. These gases alter the global climate, creating extreme weather events and causing environmental changes that harm people's health and well-being. All concerned citizens need to urge their governments to take steps that will slow the warming of the planet. Also, everyone needs to use energy wisely, consume less, and waste less.

ISSUE 05 CLIMATE CHANGE

Vocabulary & Expressions:

climate
*the usual weather conditions in a particular place
- Kuwait has a warm *climate* year-round.

erratic
*not consistent or regular
- It is difficult to live with someone whose moods are *erratic*.

reef
*a chain of rocks or coral at or near the surface of water
- Australia's Great Barrier Reef is the world's largest coral *reef*.

atoll
*a ring-shaped coral island consisting of a coral reef surrounding a lagoon
- The 1,200 coral islands of the Maldives are grouped into 26 *atolls*.

plight
*a bad condition or situation; a predicament
- The *plight* of homeless people is a major problem in large cities.

bleak
*not hopeful or encouraging
- The president apologized for rising inflation and the *bleak* economy.

cyclone
*a large, powerful, and destructive storm with very high winds that turn around continuously
- *Cyclone* Tino created severe damage to ten island nations in the Pacific Ocean in January 2020.

sound the alarm
*to warn people
- Economists have *sounded the alarm* about possible economic problems next year.

canary in the coal mine
*something that acts as an early warning of possible danger
- The idiom *canary in the coal mine* comes from the old practice of miners taking a caged canary into a coal mine. If the bird died, the miners would be alerted to the presence of dangerous gases.

buildup
*an increase in something that occurs over a period of time
- Smokers experience a *buildup* of fluid in their lungs.

greenhouse gases
*various gases, such as carbon dioxide and methane, that trap heat in the atmosphere and contribute to the warming of planet Earth
- The United Nations warns that we must reduce *greenhouse gases* so that Earth's temperature does not rise more than 2°C by 2050.

fossil fuels
*a fuel, such as coal, oil, or natural gas, formed in the earth from dead plants or animals
- Gasoline is a *fossil fuel* used in most cars today.

Open to Debate (2): 30 Global Issues

Discussion Points:

1. What do you think will happen to Tuvalu during the next thirty years? What about Hawaii?
2. How has climate change affected your country?
3. Does your country have a ministry of the environment? Do you think they do a good job?
4. What should be done to reduce the number of cars on the street?
5. Have you seen an increasing number of extreme weather events during your lifetime?
6. How does climate change affect you personally? Has it harmed your health?
7. Do you think you are good at recycling? What kinds of items do you recycle?

Read the following quotes about climate change.
Can you explain what they mean? Do you agree with the idea expressed?

8. I want you to act as if the house is on fire, because it is. Greta Thunberg
9. The future will be green or not at all. Jonathon Porritt
10. We do not inherit the earth from our ancestors; we borrow it from our children. Native American Proverb

● Current Hot Topic: Meat-Free Meals to Save the Planet?

Meat is eaten around the world, but in rich nations, eating meat is an obsession. Most people know that a diet heavy in meat increases the risk of obesity, cancer, and heart disease. However, raising cows, pigs, and chickens generates as many greenhouse gas emissions as all automobiles combined. It would be beneficial for the planet if everyone became a vegetarian. Of course, not everyone can adopt that sort of diet, but everyone can choose to have meat-free meals just one day a week. Making that choice would help planet Earth and also benefit people's health.

● For Further Discussion:

1. Do you know any vegetarians? What is their life like? Could you ever become a vegetarian?
2. Would you be willing to eat meat-free meals for just one day per week?

All types of corruption were widespread throughout the world. Adults on Earth enjoyed consorting with POWER, MONEY, AND FAME. And their insatiable thirst for more greed didn't stop there. They finally decided to fly into space for even more power, money, and fame.

On Earth, however, only kids, animals, and trees are left. They've come to live peacefully together without corruption.

The globe: I'm afraid it's too late for me to heal because self-centered adults have left such deep scars on me. But I believe time will be a great healer once they've left me alone.

Topic Preview:

How would you rank the level of corruption in your country: high, moderate, or low? When was the last time that you read about an incident of corruption? What happened? Have you personally seen any examples of corruption? What happened? What punishment should corrupt officials receive?

Dialogue:

Susan: Edward, I have a question about your country. New Zealand is always ranked as one of the least corrupt countries in the world.

Edward: Yes, that's correct.

Susan: Well, what's your secret? How does your country consistently keep corruption almost nonexistent?

Edward: Well, for one thing, we are a small country with a little more than five million people, so honesty in government and business is easier to monitor.

Susan: I see. But that can't be the only reason for the lack of corruption.

Edward: You're right. We have a department called the Serious Fraud Office that investigates any examples of corruption.

Susan: Okay. That makes sense.

Edward: We also have an Independent Police Conduct Authority, which handles all complaints regarding the police.

Susan: Well, it sounds as though New Zealand has several agencies that work hard to prevent any type of corruption.

Edward: You are absolutely correct about that. They stay on top of any problems.

Corruption

Many people think of corruption as mainly a problem in developing countries. It is assumed that highly developed countries would not need to offer money under the table to obtain a lucrative deal. However, corruption is a ubiquitous problem faced by every country in the world, including those at the height of economic power. Most people have heard of Siemens, a huge multinational conglomerate headquartered in Munich, Germany. Beginning in 2005, Siemens became embroiled in a multinational bribery scandal. The company came under legal scrutiny by both Germany and the US. The investigations eventually revealed that bribery of government officials and businesspeople was standard operating procedure for Siemens for many years. The numerous cases of bribery included $20 million paid in Israel for a contract to build power plants, $16 million in Venezuela for urban rail lines, and $14 million in China for medical equipment. In the end, Siemens paid a total of about $800 million in fines to Germany and the same amount to the US.

Corruption in government and business can occur on different scales. It can occur as *petty corruption*, which is a small-scale act of corruption that occurs, for example, when a citizen bribes a police officer. *Grand corruption* occurs at the highest levels of government and is often found in countries with dictatorial governments. *Systemic corruption* occurs widely in countries with weak governments and a culture of impunity.

Transparency International (TI) was founded in 1993 with the purpose of exposing and combating corruption around the world. Each year TI publishes the *Corruption Perceptions Index*, which ranks countries by their perceived levels of public corruption, as determined by expert assessments and opinion surveys. Often, one of the Scandinavian countries or New Zealand is considered the least corrupt country and Somalia or Sudan the most corrupt.

ISSUE 06 CORRUPTION

Vocabulary & Expressions:

under the table — *in a secret manner
- The politician was arrested for taking money *under the table*.

lucrative — *producing a lot of money or wealth; very profitable
- Smartphones are a very *lucrative* business for Samsung.

ubiquitous — *existing or being everywhere, especially at the same time
- Starbucks coffee shops are *ubiquitous* in most large cities.

conglomerate — *a large business that is made up of different kinds of companies
- The largest *conglomerates* in South Korea are Samsung Electronics, Hyundai Motor, and SK Holdings.

bribery — *the act of giving or taking something valuable, such as money, in order to get someone to do something
- In 2020, Airbus agreed to pay a record $4 billion in fines for alleged *bribery* and corruption.

standard operating procedure — *a set of fixed instructions used in a company for carrying out routine operations; abbreviated as SOP
- One reason why McDonald's is so successful is because each location follows the company's *standard operating procedure*.

power plant — *a building in which electric power is generated
- The US has about 60 nuclear *power plants*, which produce 20% of the country's electricity.

petty — *relatively minor in degree; not too serious
- Public drunkenness is considered a *petty* crime in the US.

dictatorial — *used to describe a person who tries to control other people in a forceful and unfair way
- Italy was ruled by a *dictatorial* leader during World War II.

systemic — *relating to and affecting an entire system
- Sadly, *systemic* racism still exists in some police departments.

impunity — *freedom from punishment, harm, or loss
- In some countries, rich people act with *impunity*; they are never punished for anything.

transparency — *the quality of being honest and open; not secretive
- In countries with high *transparency*, bribes are not allowed.

Scandinavian countries — *the five countries of Scandinavia: Denmark, Norway, Sweden, Finland, and Iceland
- All of the *Scandinavian countries* are on the continent of Europe, except for Iceland, which is located in the Atlantic Ocean.

Open to Debate (2): 30 Global Issues

Discussion Points:

1. The Scandinavian countries are always ranked highly on the *Corruption Perceptions Index* and other international rankings of cultural achievements. Why do you think this is true?
2. Do you know how your country ranks on the most recent edition of TI's *Corruption Perceptions Index* (available at transparency.org)? Do you think the ranking is accurate?
3. Have you read recently about any cases of corruption in your country? What happened?
4. Do you know anyone who has bribed a police officer or other government official? What happened?
5. Have you ever brought a gift to a teacher in the hope of getting a higher grade? What happened?

Read the following quotes about corruption.
Can you explain what they mean? Do you agree with the idea expressed?

6. Power tends to corrupt and absolute power corrupts absolutely. Great men are almost always bad men. Lord Acton
7. The more numerous the laws, the more corrupt the government. Tacitus

Current Hot Topic: Tax Havens and Corrupt Money

Much of the money collected through corrupt activities ends up in what are known as "tax havens" or "offshore accounts." The world got a good look at this type of secret account when the "Pandora Papers" were leaked to the press in 2021, exposing the secret financial accounts of 35 world leaders, as well as more than 100 billionaires, celebrities, and business leaders. Among them were several associates of Russian President Vladimir Putin. The shocking financial revelations in these documents were similar to those revealed in the "Panama Papers" in 2016 and the "Paradise Papers" in 2017.

For Further Discussion:

1. Where do corrupt politicians and businesspeople in your country usually hide their illegal money? Is your country considered a tax haven?
2. If you suddenly won a huge lottery, where would you put the money? Would you choose a tax haven? Which one?

— Let me show you our two labs: this is the vaccine development lab, and that is the virus development lab.
— What? I don't understand why you need a lab for virus development.
— It's as simple as that. If we don't have new viruses, we won't be able to develop proper vaccines. We have already developed thousands of new viruses!
— What if some of them escape "by mistake"? I'm scared of what would happen!
— You don't have to worry about a thing. We have all kinds of vaccines for currently developed viruses. We're ready to sell our vaccines at any time.

It's so easy to escape from this lab! It seems that researchers aren't strictly controlling us ON PURPOSE. We'll spread like wildfire and prey on people before the vaccine is available. In particular, kids and elderly people will be easy prey for us!

Topic Preview:

How did the COVID-19 pandemic affect your country? How did it affect you personally? Have you been vaccinated against the COVID-19 virus? Do you know anyone who refused to get the COVID-19 vaccine? What was their reasoning?

Dialogue:

Sarah: Hey, George, have you gotten the COVID-19 vaccine?

George: Of course! I got both shots several months ago. What about you?

Sarah: I just got my first shot. I'm scheduled to get the second one later this month.

George: Why did you wait so long? The vaccine has been available for months.

Sarah: Well, I was a little skeptical at first, but something happened to change my mind.

George: What was that?

Sarah: My uncle got COVID-19 and died from it. He was not vaccinated.

George: Oh, that's terrible! I'm sorry to hear that.

Sarah: Well, after his experience, I thought I should get it as soon as possible.

George: You made a wise decision.

COVID-19

On December 8, 2019, a Chinese accountant named Mr. Chen became ill in Wuhan, China. He was a frequent shopper at the RT-Mart, which was located near his home on the eastern bank of the Yangtze River. He preferred its modern shops with escalator ramps, so he rarely visited Wuhan's famous seafood market. However, his parents shopped at the seafood market. Before his illness, he had not traveled outside of Wuhan. Mr. Chen could not have known that his illness would eventually give him the moniker "patient zero" of COVID-19. Other COVID patients have been suggested as the first one to come down with COVID-19, but Mr. Chen remains the most likely choice according to many scientists.

COVID-19 is one member of a family of different viruses known as coronaviruses. Some of them cause the common cold; others infect animals, including bats, camels, cattle, and pangolins. But it remains to be seen exactly where the coronavirus that led to COVID-19 actually originated. Some researchers have suggested that the virus came from one of Wuhan's open-air wet markets, which are traditional markets where customers buy fresh meat and fish. Some of the animals are slaughtered on the spot. Other researchers believe that the source of the virus was a lab leak from the Wuhan Institute of Virology.

Regardless of the source, COVID-19 has infected hundreds of millions of people worldwide and has killed millions. The symptoms of the disease appear 2–14 days after exposure to the virus. The symptoms include coughing, shortness of breath or difficulty breathing, fever, chills, muscle pain, sore throat, and loss of taste or smell. Incredibly, a vaccine for COVID-19 was developed in record time, only a year after the appearance of the disease. By the end of December 2020, many countries had approved a vaccine.

ISSUE 07 COVID-19

Vocabulary & Expressions:

moniker *a name or nickname
- New York City has been given the *moniker* "The Big Apple."

come down with *to begin to suffer from an illness
- My nose is runny; I think I'm *coming down with* a cold.

remains to be seen *to be uncertain, not exactly known or decided
- It *remains to be seen* whether or not the student was lying.

open-air *located outside rather than inside a building
- The Khan El-Khalili Bazaar in Cairo is the most famous *open-air* market in the Middle East.

wet market *a market that sells fresh meat, fish, produce, and sometimes live animals, which are often slaughtered on-site
- Several countries have banned *wet markets* from selling wild animals because it is feared that they may carry disease.

slaughter *to kill an animal for food
- Most countries require that animals killed for food must be *slaughtered* in a careful and painless manner.

lab leak *a situation where a disease accidentally escapes from a laboratory
- It is impossible to prove or disprove that the COVID-19 virus came from a *lab leak*.

virology *a branch of science that studies viruses and the diseases they cause
- *Virology* focuses on the structure, classification, and evolution of viruses.

infect *to cause someone to become sick or affected by disease
- My sister has a cold; I hope she doesn't *infect* me.

exposure *the condition of coming in contact with a disease or diseased person
- My mother is a nurse; every day she has *exposure* to various sick people.

shortness of breath *difficulty breathing
- People who are not in good physical condition experience *shortness of breath* when they run quickly.

chills *an unpleasant cold feeling
- If you experience a fever and then *chills*, you may have the flu (influenza).

in record time *in the least amount of time ever
- The runner from Kenya finished the marathon *in record time*.

Open to Debate (2): 30 Global Issues

Discussion Points:

1. Do you agree that Mr. Chen is likely "patient zero," the first person to have COVID-19? Could someone else be the first person?

2. In your view, which is a more likely origin for COVID-19, an animal or a lab leak?

3. How did your government handle the COVID-19 pandemic? Do you think they did a good job?

4. Do you know anyone who got COVID-19? Do you know anyone who died from it?

5. Are there many people in your country who refuse to get the COVID-19 vaccine? What reasons do they give?

6. Do you think that people who work in certain jobs should be required to get the COVID-19 vaccine (e.g., health care workers, teachers)?

7. Do you think that rich countries have a moral obligation to help poor countries get the COVID-19 vaccine? How is your country helping?

Current Hot Topic: Anti-Vaxxers

Dick Farrel was a popular radio host and strong supporter of US President Donald Trump. When the COVID-19 pandemic began to spread throughout the world, he was skeptical. When a vaccine was developed in late 2020, he called the vaccine "a dangerous scam," and he urged his supporters to refuse the vaccine. However, in July 2021, Farrel contracted the virus himself and entered the hospital. Three weeks later, he was dead. Before passing away, he said to his friends, "Get the vaccine!" Sadly, Farrel is one of the thousands who died of COVID-19 because they were vaccine skeptics, or "anti-vaxxers."

For Further Discussion:

1. Why are some people so skeptical of vaccines? Why can't they trust the work of scientists?

2. Is vaccine skepticism common in your country? Have people demonstrated publicly against vaccines or vaccine requirements?

The last two world wars were about ideology, but now a new kind of war is on the brink of breaking out. It's a war between dollars and cryptocurrencies.

Dollar : I've dominated every aspect of people's financial lives as the global trading currency for a long time. However, I'm now being challenged by digital currencies. They look stronger than I expected, so I will need to make an alliance with the euro, yen, and yuan, if possible.

Cryptocurrency : I don't care about their coalition forces. We're able to reproduce our money endlessly, such as Citcoin and Ditcoin. In addition, we don't have to worry about inflation, unlike them. If there's a war of money, we're sure to defeat them.

Euro : The dollar is my longtime friend, so I have to support him. But I'm afraid he will think I'm his potential enemy and kill me after we achieve victory.

Yuan : I'll side with cryptocurrency because my enemy's enemy is my friend. If the US dollar is defeated, I'm going to replace it and become the standard currency.

Arms dealer : I didn't know the paradigm of war has changed. They're waging a war with money, not with weapons! Who is going to buy my weapons? I'm afraid my days of business are numbered unless I can suggest a new paradigm of war to them.

Topic Preview:

What do you know about bitcoin? Can you name any digital currencies besides bitcoin? How easy is it to buy bitcoin where you live? What do you think is the future of bitcoin and other digital currencies?

Dialogue:

Sandra: Hey Brian. What are you going to do with your Christmas bonus this year?

Brian: I'm thinking about buying some digital currency.

Sandra: You mean bitcoin?

Brian: Well, bitcoin is the most famous digital currency, but I'm thinking about buying some Dogecoin.

Sandra: You're kidding! You know that Dogecoin was created as joke by two software engineers, right?

Brian: Yeah, I know that, but I think I could still make some money in it. It has gone from less than one cent up to 73 cents this year.

Sandra: Well, it was only at 73 cents for a short time. Then it dropped very quickly.

Brian: That's true, but it's bound to go up again.

Sandra: I'm not so sure, but good luck with your investment.

Brian: Thanks. If I make a lot of money, I'll buy you a cup of coffee.

Sandra: That's all? You are such a cheapskate!

Digital Currencies

On October 31, 2008, a man named Satoshi Nakamoto posted on the Internet a fascinating article that he had written, entitled "Bitcoin: A Peer-to-Peer Electronic Cash System." The article proposed establishing a system of anonymous electronic transactions that would take place on peer-to-peer networks. The network would be called *bitcoin*, a compound of the words *bit* and *coin*. Bitcoin was designed to be a decentralized digital currency, without a central bank or single administrator. Transactions would be verified by network nodes through cryptography and recorded in a public ledger called a blockchain. People could earn bitcoins as a reward for using their computers to participate in a complicated process known as *mining*.

The entire bitcoin network would be limited to 21 million bitcoins. In 2009, Nakamoto mined the first block of bitcoin, which had a reward of 50 bitcoins. The real identity of Satoshi Nakamoto remains a mystery. The first known commercial transaction using bitcoin occurred in 2010 when computer programmer Laszlo Hanyecz bought two Papa John's pizzas for 10,000 bitcoin. Since bitcoin began to be traded, its price has fluctuated greatly. Many financial experts have called bitcoin a speculative bubble. However, economists' doubts about the value of bitcoin have not stopped people from trading it.

Bitcoin has been criticized by law enforcement authorities as a major source of payment for illegal activities, such as drug transactions. In addition, approximately one million bitcoins have been stolen from bitcoin exchanges. Still, the price of bitcoin has dramatically increased during its short history. Also, other digital currencies have arisen to compete with bitcoin, including Ethereum and Litecoin. Surprisingly, two digital currencies, Shiba Inu and Dogecoin, were both created as a joke. The value of digital currencies as an investment remains an iffy matter, and trading them is not for the faint of heart.

Note: No strict rule exists for capitalizing the word *bitcoin*. However, the *Wall Street Journal* supports using the lowercase *bitcoin* in all cases.

ISSUE 08 DIGITAL CURRENCIES

Vocabulary & Expressions:

peer-to-peer
*using a network where individual computer users can share information directly with others without relying on a central server
- Some Internet users download music through **peer-to-peer** file sharing networks; however, this action is illegal if the music is copyright.

bit
*a small unit of computer information that is the result of a choice between two alternatives, such as 1 or 0
- The word **bit** is a contraction of "binary digit."

decentralize
*to change something by taking control from one group and giving it to many people or groups
- The county school administration has been **decentralized** and moved to individual schools.

central bank
*a national bank that establishes monetary and fiscal policy and controls the money supply and interest rate
- The Bank of Korea, the **central bank** of Korea, was established in 1950.

ledger
*a book or online system that an organization uses to record information about the money it has paid and received
- Company **ledgers** are usually divided into three types: sales, purchases, and general.

remains a mystery
*continues to be unknown
- The police could not identify the body found by the river; his identity **remains a mystery**.

commercial
*having to do with the buying and selling of goods and services
- Whether you buy a cup of coffee or pay a taxi driver, you are making a **commercial** transaction.

fluctuate
*to change continually and especially to go up and down
- The price of a new company's stock often **fluctuates** greatly during the first year.

speculative
*based on guesses or ideas about what might happen rather than on facts
- Digital currency is a **speculative** investment: you could make a lot of money or lose everything.

bubble
*a state of booming economic activity, as in real estate or a stock market, that often ends in a sudden collapse
- Japan went through an economic **bubble** from 1986 to 1991, but it burst in 1992, leaving the economy ruined.

iffy
*having many uncertain or unknown qualities or conditions; not certain
- Opening a new coffee shop in my town is an **iffy** business idea because there are already so many coffee shops around here.

the faint of heart
*describing people who lack the courage or strength to face a difficult, dangerous, or risky task
- Bungee jumping is not for **the faint of heart**.

Open to Debate (2): 30 Global Issues

Discussion Points:

1. How much do you know about bitcoin? Can you name any businesses that accept it as payment?
2. Do you think that buying bitcoin is a good investment? What risks are involved in investing in bitcoin?
3. Do you have any friends or family members who own bitcoin? What do they say about this type of currency?
4. If someone gave you a gift of $1,000, how would you rather receive it: in bitcoin, gold, or your country's currency?
5. If you wanted to buy some bitcoin today, do you know where and how you could buy it?

Read the following quotes about bitcoin.
Can you explain what they mean? Do you agree with the idea expressed?

6. Bitcoin is the most important invention in the history of the world since the Internet. Roger Ver
7. Bitcoin will do to banks what email did to the postal industry. Rick Falkvinge

Current Hot Topic: Bitcoin as a National Currency

In 2021, El Salvador became the first country in the world to adopt bitcoin as its national currency. Bitcoin can now be used in any transaction, from buying a cup of coffee to renting a hotel room. The president of El Salvador, Nayib Bukele, has promoted bitcoin as a path to financial freedom for his citizens, about 70% of whom don't even have bank accounts. The president also argues that using bitcoin would make it easier for citizens to receive money from abroad. However, many economists and many Salvadorans worry that the choice of bitcoin is accompanied by great risks.

For Further Discussion:

1. Do you think that El Salvador made a wise decision in making bitcoin its national currency? What negative outcomes could the country experience?
2. Would you like to see bitcoin as a national currency in your country? What about as a second, alternative currency?

I had no friends, and I thought that drugs could be my friends. But they have become my worst enemy instead. I thought drugs would fill my emptiness, but they have actually increased my emptiness. My condition is beyond hope.

Moon: Everybody deserves a second chance. Focus on where you want to go, not where you currently are. Get your life together! I promise I will watch your back.

Topic Preview:

Is drug addiction a problem in your country nowadays? What punishment does a drug dealer receive? What countries do you think have the worst drug problems in the world? What countries have the fewest problems with illegal drugs?

Dialogue:

Patricia: Hey Kevin. What are you planning to do for your summer vacation?

Kevin: My best friend and I are planning to visit Singapore and Malaysia.

Patricia: Oh wow! That sounds awesome!

Kevin: Have you ever visited those countries?

Patricia: Not yet but I'd like to some day.

Kevin: Well, I'll show you all my photos when I return.

Patricia: Okay. By the way, just make sure you don't carry any illegal drugs into those countries.

Kevin: Why do you say that?

Patricia: Well, those countries will sentence to death any person caught carrying illegal drugs.

Kevin: Wow! They are really strict! Well, that won't be a problem for me. I have never used any illegal drugs.

Drug Abuse

After Britton Smith graduated from high school, he joined the US Army. Shortly thereafter, at age 19, he sustained a severe shoulder injury, which created continuous pain. His Army doctor prescribed for him a powerful painkiller known as an opioid. By age 22, Britton was completely addicted to the opioid. Sadly, his wife was also suffering from substance abuse. For over a decade, Britton struggled with his addiction to prescription opiods. During that time, he separated from his wife, who ultimately died due to her drug addiction, and he lost custody of his children. In 2018, Britton was arrested, jailed, and eventually turned over to a special drug rehabilitation program. The program is especially designed for veterans and provides an alternative to prison. With the help of this program, Britton was able to achieve recovery. He is now remarried and living a productive life.

Unfortunately, success stories like Britton's are few and far between. For every person suffering from drug addiction, there are hundreds more who end up losing their lives to the disease. According to the *United Nations World Drug Report*, more than 35 million people worldwide suffer from drug use disorders while only one in seven people receive treatment. It is estimated that more than 5% of the global population aged 15–64 use drugs in a year.

Experts estimate that more than 350,000 people worldwide die annually from dependence on alcohol or illicit drugs, including cocaine, heroin, amphetamines, opiods, and cannabis. In some countries, drug overdoses rank highly among the leading causes of death. The scourge of illegal drugs leads to other crimes, including murder and various types of theft. A study in the UK found that 85% of shoplifting, 70% of burglaries, and 54% of robberies were committed to support a person's addiction to illegal drugs.

ISSUE 09 DRUG ABUSE

Vocabulary & Expressions:

sustain
*to experience or deal with something bad or unpleasant; to suffer
- My father was in a terrible car accident; he *sustained* several broken bones.

opioid
*a powerful drug that is used to relieve pain, dull the senses, or produce a feeling of intoxication
- *Opioids* include legally prescribed drugs, such as oxycodone and fentanyl, as well as illegal drugs, such as heroin and cocaine.

substance abuse
*excessive use of a drug, such as alcohol, opioids, or prescribed painkillers; also known as *substance use disorder*
- *Substance abuse* is a nicer way of saying "drug addiction."

prescription
*a medicine that is ordered by a doctor as a remedy
- Some simple drugs, such as aspirin, can be purchased by anyone, but *prescription* drugs can only be bought with a doctor's order.

custody
*the legal right to take care of a child, such as a child whose parents get divorced
- In cases of divorce, judges often award *custody* of the children to the mother because she is the primary caregiver.

rehabilitation
*the process of restoring someone back to a normal, healthy condition after an illness, injury, or drug addiction; also called *rehab*
- Ben Affleck has entered a *rehabilitation* clinic several times due to a problem with alcohol.

veteran
*a person who has served in a military force, especially one who has fought in a war
- Well-known actor Morgan Freeman is a *veteran* of the US Air Force.

few and far between
*few in number and not frequently seen; rare
- Nowadays, most movies are just average; truly great movies are *few and far between*.

dependence
*addiction to drugs or alcohol
- My uncle took strong painkillers for his back injury; sadly, he developed a *dependence* on them and had to go into rehab.

illicit
*not legally permitted; unlicensed or unlawful
- My cousin was arrested for selling *illicit* copies of a new software.

cannabis
*another name for marijuana
- More than 30 US states allow the medical use of *cannabis* if the user has a doctor's recommendation.

scourge
*someone or something that causes a great amount of trouble or suffering
- Violent crime is a terrible *scourge* in many of the world's largest cities.

Open to Debate (2): 30 Global Issues

Discussion Points:

1. Why do people start taking illegal drugs? Why can't they quit?
2. Are illegal drugs a problem in your country? Which types of drugs?
3. If someone in your country wanted to buy illegal drugs, where would they find them?
4. Do you personally know anyone who is addicted to drugs? What is their life like?
5. Do you consider alcohol a drug? At what point does a person become an alcoholic?

Read the following quotes about illegal drugs.
Can you explain what they mean? Do you agree with the idea expressed?

6. There's not a drug on Earth that can make life meaningful. Sarah Kane
7. Drugs take you to hell, disguised as heaven. Donald Lyn Frost
8. When everything seems like an uphill struggle, just think of the view from the top. Unknown
9. Recovery is hard. Regret is harder. Brittany Burgunder

Current Hot Topic: Should Drugs Be Decriminalized?

Countries deal with the issue of illegal drugs in various ways. In Malaysia and Singapore, you can be executed if you are caught with illegal drugs. You will be arrested and sent to prison in many other countries. However, a few countries have actually decriminalized drugs. In 2001, Portugal legalized the use of all illegal drugs, including possession of small amounts. Nowadays, no one in Portugal is arrested or imprisoned for drug possession. The country also created rapid and effective treatment programs for drug addicts. Many countries around the world are now wondering if they should follow Portugal's example.

For Further Discussion:

1. What punishment do you think is appropriate for drug dealers? What about drug users?
2. Would you support the decriminalization of all illegal drugs in your country? What about decriminalizing only marijuana?

Inspector: Did you agree to have an assisted suicide?
Patient: Yes, but I didn't want it at first. The doctor "threatened" me to get me to agree.
Inspector: Did you force him to accept it?
Doctor: No, I just "advised" him about how to find a COMFORTABLE END to his life.
Inspector: Did you sign your name on the paper by yourself?
Patient: No, I didn't.
Doctor: I did it for him because he was TOO FEEBLE to hold a pen.

Topic Preview:

Should physicians be allowed to help people end their lives? What happens in your country if someone is in a coma and cannot recover? Is their family permitted to "pull the plug" and let the person die? Would you want to die if you are unconscious and cannot recover?

Dialogue:

Nancy: Joshua, I heard that your grandfather was seriously injured in a car accident. I'm sorry to hear about that.

Joshua: Thank you, Nancy. Yes, he has been unconscious now for two months.

Nancy: That's too bad. It's so sad.

Joshua: Well, he does have an "advance health care directive," so we may have to use that provision.

Nancy: What is an advance health care directive?

Joshua: It's a legal document in which a person specifies how they want to be treated in case they become severely disabled.

Nancy: What did your grandfather say in this document?

Joshua: He said that he did not want his life prolonged by machines if he were unconscious for a long time.

Nancy: I see. Well, it looks as though your family may have to make a decision about ending his treatment.

Joshua: Yes, that's right. My grandmother has said that if he has not regained consciousness after another month, she wants the doctors to withhold treatment and let him pass away.

Nancy: Well, that's so sad. You and your grandfather will be in my thoughts.

Euthanasia

In 2012, a pair of 45-year-old twin brothers received some bad news. They were slowly going blind. They were born deaf, but now it was clear that they were going to lose their sight as well. Apart from their deafness and impending blindness, they were in good physical health. However, the thought that they would never be able to see each other was unbearable. They had worked together, lived together, and been inseparable their entire lives. Therefore, they sought permission to end their lives legally. Fortunately for them, they lived in Belgium, one of the few countries in the world that allows euthanasia for nonterminally ill patients. On the day of their death, they were happy and calm as they were euthanized by lethal injection.

The word *euthanasia* refers to the practice of intentionally ending a person's life to relieve pain and suffering. Euthanasia is legal in only a handful of countries, where the rules vary greatly. The practice of euthanasia is usually divided into three types. *Voluntary euthanasia* is conducted with the informed consent of the patient. In some cases, physicians inject a patient with a lethal drug, an act that is called *active euthanasia*. This type of euthanasia is very controversial and is only allowed in a few countries. *Passive euthanasia* occurs where lifesaving treatment is withheld at the patient's request.

Nonvoluntary euthanasia occurs where the consent of the patient is not possible. For example, if a patient is in a coma with no hope of recovery, his family may request that medical treatment be withheld.

Involuntary euthanasia is conducted against the will of the patient. This practice is widely opposed and is regarded as a crime in all legal jurisdictions. However, it has been legal in the past, most notably in Nazi Germany during World War II.

ISSUE 10 EUTHANASIA

Vocabulary & Expressions:

impending *happening or likely to happen soon
- My father will soon become 65; he is a little concerned about his *impending* retirement.

unbearable *too bad, harsh, or extreme to be accepted or endured
- The summer heat in the Sahara Desert is *unbearable*; it's difficult to endure for more than a few minutes.

inseparable *difficult to separate; seemingly always together
- My grandparents were *inseparable*; people always saw them together.

terminally ill *having a disease that cannot be cured and will certainly cause death
- Steve Jobs died at age 56; he was *terminally ill* with cancer.

lethal injection *using a special needle to force a chemical substance that causes death into a person's body
- The United States was the first country to develop *lethal injection* as a means of execution for criminals.

handful *a small amount or number
- Bob invited 25 people to his birthday party, but only a *handful* of people came.

voluntary *doing something because you want to and not because you are forced to
- When Sally left her job, it was a *voluntary* decision; she was not fired.

informed consent *a formal agreement that a patient signs to give permission for a medical procedure after having been told about the risks and benefits
- In most cases, physicians must get the *informed consent* of a patient before performing surgery on that person.

nonvoluntary *referring to cases of medical procedures where a patient is unable to agree to the procedure because of physical or mental disabilities
- About 20% of the cases of euthanasia in the Netherlands are performed without the request of the patient, so these are cases of *nonvoluntary* euthanasia.

coma *a condition resembling deep sleep that is caused by sickness or injury
- My cousin was in a *coma* for two weeks after he was injured in a car accident.

involuntary *referring to an act that is forced on a person without their agreement
- In 1939, Adolf Hitler enacted a program of *involuntary* euthanasia, whose goal was to kill physically or mentally disabled people.

jurisdiction *a place where government officials have the power, right, or authority to interpret and apply the law
- Bank robbery is considered part of federal *jurisdiction*; parking tickets are considered part of city *jurisdiction*.

Open to Debate (2): 30 Global Issues

Discussion Points:

1. Has the issue of euthanasia ever been debated in your country's congress? What was the outcome?
2. Do you think euthanasia should be allowed in your country? Under what circumstances?
3. If you were in a coma for a long time, would you want to be kept alive by machines?
4. Do you know anyone who went into a coma? What happened to them?

Read the following quotes about euthanasia.
Can you explain what they mean? Do you agree with the idea expressed?

5. The killing of a disabled person is not "compassionate." It is not "euthanasia." It is murder. Stella Young
6. Euthanasia is a grave violation of the law of God, since it is the deliberate and morally unacceptable killing of a human person. Pope John Paul II
7. The "right to die" can easily become the "duty to die." Peter Saunders

Current Hot Topic: The Suicide Pod

Switzerland has recently legalized a new way to die by assisted suicide through the use of a "suicide pod." The "pod" or "capsule" looks similar to a small car. Persons who wish to end their life must first take an online survey to determine if they are making the decision of their own free will. If they are approved, they will be allowed to enter the pod. After answering a few questions, they can press a button that will flood the interior with nitrogen, which will quickly reduce the oxygen level. Within 30 seconds, they will die a peaceful death.

For Further Discussion:

1. Do you think the suicide pod should be available in your country? What are the pros and cons?
2. Have you ever known anyone who talked about suicide? What happened to them?

Man in the cage: To understand what life is like for caged chickens, I've put myself in their shoes. Now I finally know how they feel. From now on, I'll be a vegan and an advocate for animal rights until I die.

— Now we're free, but I'm afraid they will cage us again soon.
— Cage us again? What are you talking about? There are laws now against animal cruelty!
— Yes, people made the laws, but they seldom abide by those laws.
— If they lock us up again, I'll take my life immediately.
— You don't have to hurry to your death. Whether or not we're caged again, we're destined to be slaughtered for food in a couple of months.
— Really? Oh my God, please put the fear of God into these merciless men!

Topic Preview:

Do you know how cows, pigs, and chickens are raised in your country? Have you ever visited a farm in your country? Would you be interested in visiting a slaughterhouse to see how animals are killed for food? Do you know anyone who is a vegetarian? What are their reasons for choosing that lifestyle?

Dialogue:

Kenneth: Michelle, are you coming to our dinner party after class on Friday?

Michelle: Well, maybe. Where will the party be held?

Kenneth: It'll be at Outback Steakhouse on Main Street.

Michelle: Oh, I'm not sure I can come. You know I'm a vegetarian, right?

Kenneth: Yes, I knew that, but Outback has menu items for vegetarians.

Michelle: Really? Like what?

Kenneth: They have salads, broccoli, mixed vegetables, baked potatoes, bread, and desserts.

Michelle: Okay. Well, I'll think about going. I'll let you know on Friday morning.

Kenneth: By the way, may I ask why you chose to be a vegetarian?

Michelle: I just don't like the way that animals are raised and processed for food through factory farming.

Kenneth: I see. Well, I respect your opinion. I hope you'll join us on Friday.

Factory Farming

About 10,000 years ago, humans began the practice of domestication of animals. Some animals, such as cows, pigs, and chickens, were domesticated for food; others, such as dogs and cats, were domesticated to become companion animals. For many centuries, the process of raising animals for food was conducted on small family farms. However, in 1947, the Agriculture Act in Britain encouraged farmers to increase output by using new technology in order to reduce the country's reliance on imported meat. In the mid-60s, the United States and other industrialized countries began "intensive animal farming," also known as "industrial livestock production," of beef and dairy cattle, pigs, and chickens. However, this process later became known as "factory farming," a pejorative term used by opponents of the practice. The mass production of animals for food was aided by the use of vitamin supplements, antibiotics, vaccines, and chemicals.

Nowadays in many countries, animals that are used for food live on massive factory farms where they're crammed into small cages or other enclosures. They are given so little space that they cannot even turn around or lie down comfortably. Most of these factory-farmed animals have been genetically manipulated to produce more milk or eggs or to grow larger than they would under natural conditions. Some chickens and cows become so unnaturally large that they can hardly stand up. These animals will never raise their families, build nests, or do anything that they would naturally do in the wild.

How should humans respond to factory farming? Many people say there's no problem as long as the animals are treated humanely. However, other people choose to become a vegetarian, vegan, or pescatarian. Organizations like Mercy for Animals and the Humane Society try to educate people about the evils of factory farming and convince them to become vegans.

ISSUE 11 FACTORY FARMING

Vocabulary & Expressions:

domestication
*the act or process of taming an animal for human use or companionship
- The *domestication* of dogs took place about 15,000 years ago.

industrialized
*describing modernized countries that have built factories and businesses
- The Industrial Revolution in 18th-century Britain led to a period of *industrialization* in Europe and North America.

livestock
*animals, such as cows, horses, and pigs, that are kept or raised, especially on a farm and for profit
- Sheep became some of the first *livestock*, around 12,000 years ago.

pejorative
*describing words that are insulting to someone or something; expressing criticism
- The word "Yankee" was first used by the British military as a *pejorative* term for Americans.

cram
*to push or force someone or something into a space that is tight or crowded
- During evening rush hour, many people are *crammed* into the subway in Tokyo.

manipulate
*to control or influence something or someone cleverly or skillfully
- Most modern breeds of dogs have been created in the last 150 years by dog breeders who cleverly *manipulated* the dog's genetic structure.

the wild
*an uncultivated, free, or natural place
- Ginseng can be cultivated, but many people prefer ginseng from *the wild*.

humanely
*in a manner that is kind or gentle to people or animals
- Criminals should be put in prison, but they should still be treated *humanely*.

vegetarian
*a person who does not eat meat
- *Vegetarians* eat vegetables, fruits, grains, nuts, and sometimes eggs or dairy products.

vegan
*a person who does not eat any food that comes from animals, including eggs, milk, and honey
- *Vegans* will not use any animal products, including leather.

pescatarian
*a vegetarian who eats fish but no other kinds of meat
- For much of his life, Steve Jobs was a *pescatarian*; he would eat fish but not beef, pork, or chicken.

evils
*something that brings sorrow, trouble, or destruction
- Every country has to deal with the *evils* of poverty.

Open to Debate (2): 30 Global Issues

Discussion Points:

1. Is the issue of factory farming a controversial topic in your country?
2. What governmental organization in your country oversees food production? Do you think they do a good job?
3. Have you ever visited a farm or a slaughterhouse? What did you learn?
4. Do you have any friends who are vegetarians or vegans? Are there any vegan restaurants in your city?
5. Do you think you could ever become a vegetarian or vegan? How about for just one day per week?

Read the following quotes about factory farming.
Can you explain what they mean? Do you agree with the idea expressed?

6. Animals run no risk of going to hell; they are there already. Victor Hugo
7. If slaughterhouses had glass walls, we would all be vegetarian.
   Paul McCartney

Current Hot Topic: Factory Farming and the Environment

Factory farming not only involves the mistreatment of animals, but it also causes extensive damage to the environment. Factory farms contribute to air pollution by releasing harmful compounds, such as hydrogen sulfide, ammonia, and methane. Methane also contributes to global warming. Animal waste contains traces of salt and heavy metals, which can end up in bodies of water. Destroying forests to create pastures for animal grazing and feed crops is estimated to release 2.4 billion tons of CO_2 every year. Factory farms also consume huge amounts of fresh water, amounting to billions of gallons of water per day.

For Further Discussion:

1. Do you think factory farming has contributed to environmental pollution in your country? In what ways?
2. Nowadays some companies, such as Beyond Meat, are producing meat-like products made from plants. Have you eaten this type of product? Do you think it's the wave of the future?

Gender equality is the ultimate goal in our generation. It will help abolish poverty, create a more equal economy, and a fairer society. Regardless of our sex and age, we will all live happily together. If elected, I'll be pouring all my energy into this purpose.

In the future, there will be no female leaders. There'll just be leaders.

I'm wondering how she'll keep her promises. Every presidential candidate vowed to achieve those goals, only to fail.

I suspect her words are just the empty rhetoric of politics.

Let's make a law that dictates that every man and woman must become a FEMINIST. Period.

Topic Preview:

Do you think that men and women in your country have achieved gender equality? Do you think that women in your country earn just as much as men doing the same job? Has your country ever had a female president? What percentage of your teachers have been women?

Dialogue:

Melissa: Andrew, why do you think the United States has never had a woman president?

Andrew: I'm not sure I have the answer. Hillary Clinton ran for president in 2016, but she lost.

Melissa: Yeah, I know. I was sad that day. But you will eventually have a woman president.

Andrew: Yeah, I'm sure it will happen, but I don't know when.

Melissa: Well, in New Zealand, we've already had three women prime ministers.

Andrew: Wow! That's amazing. I had no idea.

Melissa: It's true. Jenny Shipley became our first prime minister back in 1997.

Andrew: Well, we Americans are behind the times.

Melissa: Yes, but you will eventually catch up.

Andrew: I hope you are right, and I hope it happens sooner than later.

Gender Equality

Recently, an organization dedicated to gender equality asked women from around the world to share real-life situations where they experienced gender discrimination. The response was shocking and overwhelming. One woman wrote, "When I was in college and a professor attempted to rape my classmate, we reported it to our homeroom teacher. She told us, 'Forget about it. These things happen in women's colleges.'" Another said, "The day of my birth, my grandmother cried because I was the third girl child born to my parents." Another girl wrote, "My college library is usually open till midnight. However, girls are not allowed in the library beyond 6:00 pm." These outrageous events represent a small sampling of the discrimination that women and girls experience on a daily basis.

The examples above seem inconsequential compared to the violence that women experience daily. About one in twenty girls between the ages of 15 and 19—around 13 million—have experienced forced sexual relations. Hundreds of millions of girls are still subjected to child marriage, even though it has been internationally recognized as a human rights violation. However, there are hopeful signs that women are standing up to defy societal restrictions against them in places where traditional male chauvinism prevails. A young woman from Bangladesh named Nasima Akter decided to become a surfer in spite of the disapproval of her husband and the majority of the male population of her country. However, when she defeated male competitors in several tournaments, some of her fellow citizens began to change their minds.

Gender equality will not be achieved, experts say, until average people become vocal advocates for it. You must learn about gender equality and educate others about it. You have to speak up if you witness sexism and use social media as your platform to influence others.

ISSUE 12 GENDER EQUALITY

Vocabulary & Expressions:

real-life
*happening in the real world rather than in a story
- The COVID-19 pandemic has brought *real-life* tragedy to many families.

gender discrimination
*treating a person or group unfairly based on their sex and especially against women; also known as *sex discrimination*
- An employer who fires an employee because she's pregnant is guilty of *gender discrimination*.

overwhelming
*overpowering in effect or strength; so strong in force that one finds it difficult to resist
- When my grandmother died, my grandfather's grief was so *overwhelming* that he hardly left his house for a year.

outrageous
*extremely annoying, insulting, or shameful
- The politician blamed his *outrageous* behavior at the party on having drunk too much alcohol.

inconsequential
*unimportant, insignificant, especially when contrasted with something that is very serious
- My bicycle accident on the way to school seemed *inconsequential* when I learned that my grandfather had cancer.

stand up
*to take a firm position in favor of what one thinks is right
- Wise people *stand up* to support women who enter politics.

defy
*to refuse to obey something or someone
- In traditional societies, only a very brave woman will *defy* her husband's orders.

male chauvinism
*the belief of some males that men are superior to women
- Because of *male chauvinism*, women in the United States did not get the right to vote until 1920.

vocal
*expressing opinions in a public and forceful way
- My father is a *vocal* critic of the new president.

advocate
*a person who argues for or supports an idea, plan, or person
- If you are accused of a crime, you will need a lawyer, who will be your *advocate* in court.

sexism
*unfair treatment of people because of their sex, especially unfair treatment of women
- Asking women why they aren't married or don't have children is just one example of the *sexism* that women face every day.

platform
*a place, means, or opportunity to communicate ideas or information to a group of people
- Most modern companies use social media as a *platform* to reach consumers with new products.

Open to Debate (2): 30 Global Issues

Discussion Points:

1. Have you, or someone you know, experienced gender-based violence or discrimination? What happened?
2. What percentage of lawmakers in your country are women? Would you like to see a 50-50 ratio?
3. What percentage of CEOs in your country are women? Do you think the ideal percentage is 50%?
4. Does your country have a traditional preference for boy babies? Would you consider it a disappointment if you had three daughters?

Read the following quotes about gender equality.
Can you explain what they mean? Do you agree with the idea expressed?

5. Achieving gender equality requires the engagement of women and men, girls and boys. It is everyone's responsibility. Ban Ki-Moon
6. I am not the woman president of Harvard; I am the president of Harvard. Drew Gilpin Faust, first woman president of Harvard (2007–2018)
7. Men are afraid that women will laugh at them. Women are afraid that men will kill them. Margaret Atwood

Current Hot Topic: Global Gender Gap Report

In order to measure worldwide gender equality in a scientific manner, the World Economic Forum (WEC) began publishing the *Global Gender Gap Report* in 2006. The annual report examines four areas of inequality between men and women in more than 150 countries:

- Economic participation and opportunity, including jobs and salaries
- Educational attainment, including access to basic and higher education levels
- Political empowerment, including women involved in political decision-making
- Health and survival, including life expectancy

The WEC estimates that it will take more than 130 years, on average, for the world to achieve gender equality.

For Further Discussion:

1. Do you know where your country ranks on the current *Global Gender Gap Report* (see weforum.org)? Do you think the ranking is accurate?
2. What are the most important steps your country can take to bridge the gender gap? Do you support politicians who promise to improve the gender gap?

China: I have grown big enough to be the number one superpower in the world. To decide who the top superpower is, I challenge you to a duel.

USA: I've never thought that you could be my rival, but I accept your challenge.

UN: Wait a minute! This fight is too risky because one of you is destined to lose your life. Why don't we determine the top superpower by comparing national income per capita? Isn't that easier and safer?

USA: I agree. We're almost $80,000 per capita, and you are $10,000. Right?

China: You're using last year's statistics. This year, we're at $100,000.

USA: How is it possible to go from $10,000 to $100,000 overnight? You must have rigged the statistics!

China: Don't get us wrong. This year, half of our population hit the numbers in the lottery, and the other half hit the jackpot on a slot machine.

Russia: Alas! If it were not for the war with Ukraine, we might be able to compete with them for the position of top superpower.

Topic Preview:

Why do countries like China, Russia, and the United States continually compete with each other? Which powerful nations is your country most closely allied with? Do you think these alliances should continue? What do you think are the chances that we will have a world war during this century?

Dialogue:

Margaret: Steven, you're majoring in political science, right?

Steven: Yes, I am. Why do you ask?

Margaret: Well, I'm wondering if you can you tell me why President Putin of Russia started a war in Ukraine.

Steven: Oh, that has a lot to do with the history of the two countries.

Margaret: What do you mean?

Steven: Well, there are a lot of Russian speakers in Ukraine, and Putin considers Russians and Ukrainians as brothers. He believes that they should all be one country.

Margaret: Well, it seems that most Ukrainians don't agree with that idea.

Steven: Yeah, you're right. The Ukrainians are a strong people, and they will fight hard to keep their independence.

Margaret: I just hope that the war doesn't spill over into Europe, which would get NATO and the United States involved.

Steven: You are so right. That sort of conflict between great powers would lead to disaster. We certainly don't need a war among superpowers.

Great Power Conflicts

Scarborough Shoal and Democracy Reef are two rocks located in a shoal in the South China Sea. They clearly fall within the EEZ of the Philippines. These rocks may seem insignificant, but they were the site of a major international confrontation in 2012, when China seized the area, while engaging in a standoff with Philippine maritime vessels. The United States attempted to broker an agreement to de-escalate tensions in the area, but the effort failed. A UN-backed international court upheld the sovereign rights of the Philippines in the area, but China rejected the court's decision. Meanwhile, China also claims ownership of much of the Spratly Islands and has even built several airports on the rocks.

Europe also is the site of a major territorial dispute. Crimea is a peninsula located along the Black Sea and is considered part of Ukraine. In 2014, the Russian military annexed Crimea, which was home to many pro-Russian separatists. However, Russia's move was declared illegitimate by Western governments. In late 2021, Russia amassed more than 100,000 soldiers on its border with Ukraine. US President Joe Biden warned Russian President Vladimir Putin not to invade Ukraine. Putin warned that Ukraine must never be admitted to NATO. On February 24, 2022, Russia invaded Ukraine, but the Ukrainians fought hard to maintain their independence.

Recently, a poll was conducted among 50 international experts. About 60% of them believed that the risk of international war has increased in the last decade. The experts estimated that there was a 5% chance of a nuclear war killing at least 80 million people in the next 20 years. Other experts predicted that there is a 1% chance of nuclear extinction of the human race in the 21st century. All of the great powers already have the capability of conducting cyberwarfare.

ISSUE 13 GREAT POWER CONFLICTS

Vocabulary & Expressions:

shoal — *a place where an ocean, lake, or river is shallow
- Ships must be very careful around *shoals* so that they don't crash into them.

EEZ — *exclusive economic zone, a 200-mile (322-km) area from a country's coast, where it has special rights for economic development
- When two countries have overlapping *EEZs*, they have to negotiate an agreement about the size of their *EEZs*.

standoff — an argument, contest, or confrontation in which there is no winner
- The Battle of Monmouth in 1778 was a *standoff*; neither the British nor the Americans won the battle.

de-escalate — *to reduce the level or intensity of a crisis, argument, or confrontation
- Police officers are taught to *de-escalate* dangerous confrontations.

uphold — *to judge a legal decision to be correct
- Accused people do not have to talk to the police; courts have *upheld* this right.

sovereign — *self-governing, independent
- Jamaica became a *sovereign* country in 1962; it was no longer governed by Britain.

annex — *to add an area or region to a country or state; to take control of a territory or place
- The United States *annexed* Texas in 1845.

separatist — *a member of a group of people who want to separate from their country and form a new country
- Many people of Catalonia are *separatists*; they want to separate from Spain.

illegitimate — *not accepted by the law as rightful and legal
- Any contract signed by a child is *illegitimate*; only adults can sign contracts.

amass — *to gather, collect, or accumulate a large amount or number of something
- By saving almost all of his money, my father *amassed* a small fortune for his retirement.

NATO — *the North Atlantic Treaty Organization, a military alliance of European countries, the US, and Canada
- When *NATO* was first formed in 1949, it had 12 members; now it has more than 30.

extinction — *the state or situation that results when something, such as a plant or animal species, has died out completely
- The dinosaurs are fascinating creatures, but unfortunately, they suffered *extinction* millions of years ago.

cyberwarfare — *computer-based attacks on a network or other digital system to harm a military or other enemy
- Using *cyberwarfare*, even small countries can successfully attack large countries.

Open to Debate (2): 30 Global Issues

Discussion Points:

1. Why are some great powers so aggressive in their international relations?
2. What do you think can be done to reduce international tensions? How can your country play a part?
3. Are you personally afraid that an international war might break out during your lifetime?

Read the following quotes about war.
Can you explain what they mean? Do you agree with the idea expressed?

4. When the rich wage war, it's the poor who die. Jean-Paul Sartre
5. War does not determine who is right—only who is left. Unknown
6. I don't oppose all wars. What I am opposed to is a dumb war. What I am opposed to is a rash war. Barack Obama
7. War is evil, but it is often the lesser evil. George Orwell
8. Refusing to fight for what someone thinks is right isn't an act of cowardice. It's the realization that wars are pointless. Unknown
9. Today the real test of power is not capacity to make war but capacity to prevent it. Unknown

Current Hot Topic: Cyberwarfare

The Colonial Pipeline is an American oil pipeline system that carries gasoline to the southeastern United States. On May 7, 2021, the company suffered a powerful ransomware cyberattack that completely shut down the system. Left with few choices, the company paid the requested ransom of 75 bitcoin ($4.4 million). Eventually, the system was restored. Around the same time, the same hackers attacked Brenntag, a German chemical company. This company also ended up paying $4.4 million to gain access to their files. This type of ransomware attack provides the world with a small glimpse of what a future cyberwar might be like.

For Further Discussion:

1. Has your country faced any ransomware attacks? What happened?
2. Do you think companies should pay the ransom demanded by hackers? What other options do they have?

Topic Preview:

What do you know about the issue of human trafficking? Who do you think is trafficked more, men or women? Does human trafficking ever occur in your country? In what situations? If you needed a kidney transplant, would you be willing to travel to another country to get one?

Dialogue:

Lisa: Paul, how is your cousin doing? I heard he was very sick.

Paul: He's not doing very well, Lisa. He needs a kidney transplant.

Lisa: Oh, that's too bad. Can anyone in your family donate a kidney?

Paul: Well, we've all been tested, and none of us are a good match.

Lisa: I see. Well, I guess he's on a long waiting list for a kidney.

Paul: Yeah, but he's getting desperate. He told me that he's even considering going to India for a transplant.

Lisa: Oh my! I've read about "transplant tourism," but it doesn't sound like a good idea to me.

Paul: Yeah, I told him that. It also sounds like a form of human trafficking to me.

Lisa: I agree. You have no idea how they got the kidneys for transplant.

Paul: Exactly! I think I've convinced him to wait his turn on the list.

Human Trafficking

When she was 22 years old, Luiza Karimova left her home in Uzbekistan and travelled to Kyrgyzstan to look for work. However, without a Kyrgyz ID or university degree, she struggled to find a job. She thought she had a change of luck when a woman offered her a job as a restaurant server in Bishkek. However, her situation took a turn for the worse after she arrived in Bishkek, along with other women. Their employer took away their passports. Then all of them were given fake passports and put on a plane to Dubai.

As soon as the women arrived, they were locked up in an apartment building. They were forced to work in a nightclub as sex slaves. For 18 months, Karimova endured this hell on earth. One day, she saw a police car, and she decided to let the police arrest her. She spent a year in jail and was deported because of her fake ID. However, she filed a police report, and three of the traffickers were captured. Later, Karimova began working for Podruga, an organization that assists women who are victims of human trafficking. Nowadays, she works to prevent other women from falling into the trap of human trafficking.

The statistics about human trafficking reveal a horrendous practice that enslaves millions of people. It is estimated that between 20 million and 40 million people are living in modern-slavery today. Understanding the full scope of human trafficking is difficult because the majority of cases go undetected. About 70% of enslaved people are women and girls. The total revenue from human trafficking tops $150 billion a year, most of which comes from sexual exploitation. Advanced countries are not immune from this scourge. About 50,000 people are trafficked into the US each year.

ISSUE 14 HUMAN TRAFFICKING

Vocabulary & Expressions:

change of luck — the shift of a person's series of bad experiences into good experiences, or vice versa
- My uncle's business lost money for several years, but then he had a *change of luck* and became very successful.

server — a person who serves food or drink in a restaurant
- Older people sometimes use the terms *waiter* and *waitress*, but most modern people use the term *server* as a gender-neutral term.

take a turn for the worse — to become more unfavorable, difficult, unpleasant, or painful
- My grandfather seemed to be getting well, but suddenly he *took a turn for the worse*.

hell on earth — a terrible or extremely unpleasant situation or circumstance
- This office has been *hell on earth* ever since the new manager came.

deport — to force a person who is not a citizen to leave a country
- If a country discovers anyone with a fake passport, they are immediately *deported*.

victim — a person who is attacked, injured, robbed, killed, or cheated by someone else
- My aunt was the *victim* of a crime recently; her purse was stolen.

human trafficking — a crime that involves forcing a person to provide labor or services
- Victims of *human trafficking* are deceived by false promises of a good job, a stable life, or even love, but are forced to work under terrible conditions.

horrendous — extremely bad or unpleasant; horrible, dreadful
- Some countries still use the death penalty for the most *horrendous* crimes.

scope — the area, amount, or range covered, reached, or viewed
- The full *scope* of the crime was not known until the police discovered the secret video.

undetected — not observed or noticed by anyone
- An American spy lived in Russia and was *undetected* for a long time.

exploitation — using another person or group for selfish purposes
- Most modern countries have strong labor unions that prevent the *exploitation* of workers.

immune — not influenced or affected by something
- Religious people are not *immune* from participating in criminal activity just because they are religious.

●●●● *Open to Debate (2): 30 Global Issues*

● Discussion Points:

1. Are there many foreign workers in your country? Do you think that any of them have been trafficked?
2. Why are women and girls the most trafficked people?
3. What punishment do you think is appropriate for human traffickers?
4. If you saw someone that you thought was being trafficked, what would you do?

Read the following quotes about human trafficking.
Can you explain what they mean? Do you agree with the idea expressed?

5. Slavery was abolished 150 years ago, and yet there are more people in slavery today than any other time in our history. Unknown
6. You may choose to look the other way, but you can never say again that you did not know. William Wilberforce
7. If slavery is not wrong, nothing is wrong. Abraham Lincoln
8. Culture is no excuse for abuse. Davinder Kaur

● Current Hot Topic: Trafficking in Human Organs

Trafficking in bodily organs is a form of human trafficking. In some cases, a person agrees to sell an organ, although he may get little money for it. In other cases, the victim is forced into giving up an organ. Finally, some victims have an organ removed without their knowledge while being treated for another medical problem. Migrant workers, unemployed people, poor people, and homeless persons are especially vulnerable to organ theft. The commercial trade of human organs is illegal in all countries except Iran. The typical price for a kidney on the black market ranges from $1,000 to $5,000.

● For Further Discussion:

1. Do you know anyone who has had an organ transplant? Where did the organ come from?
2. Would you be willing to donate a kidney to help a member of your family? Would you ever sell a kidney if you needed money?

If the word GREED did not exist, there would be enough food to eat, clothes to wear, houses to live in, and money to spend around the world. Therefore, our government has decided to get rid of the word GREED in the dictionary and has declared that using the word is illegal. If somebody uses the word, he will be liable for strict punishment. As a result, greedy people, especially the superrich, have begun to share their riches with needy people.

That's the best law I've ever seen! I'll support the government forever.

Govt.: We tried to narrow the gap between the rich and poor, only to fail. Now ridding the rich of greedy desires is the best recipe to achieve our goals.

The rich: This is the worst law I've ever seen! We'll try to repeal the law from now on. If we don't succeed, we'll at least lobby for reform of this unjust law.

Topic Preview:

Have you ever skipped a meal because you didn't have enough money to buy food? How did you feel? How does your country help poor and homeless people who don't have enough food? If you saw a child who was weak due to a lack of food, what would you do?

Dialogue:

Linda: Hey, Mark. Did you see that lady begging for money this morning at the subway entrance?

Mark: Yes, I did. She looked very thin. I felt really sorry for her, but I didn't know if I should give her any money or not.

Linda: Yeah, I always wonder if it's a good idea to give money. Shouldn't the government be helping people like that?

Mark: Of course, but who knows what her situation is? Maybe she is sacrificing what little she has to help her children.

Linda: Yeah, that could be true.

Mark: Maybe we should just buy her a bag of groceries and give it to her.

Linda: Hmmm… that's a good idea. Then we'll know that she's really getting some food.

Mark: Okay. Let's stop by the supermarket today after work.

Linda: Yeah, let's do it. It's so sad that even in a developed country like ours, there are still people who don't have enough food.

Mark: You are so right. It's even worse in developing countries. The United Nations should do everything it can to solve this problem.

Hunger and Malnourishment

The popular film series entitled *Hunger Games* depicts a dystopian future, where people fight for existence and even for food to eat. However, this sort of situation exists in the real world. Consider the case of an Ethiopian woman named Abiyot. On many nights, she cried herself to sleep, out of despair for her inability to feed her six children. Her husband had abandoned the family and remarried. To add insult to injury, she had been laid off from her part-time job. Not only had her job come to an end, but the breakfast and lunches that her children used to depend on through the government's welfare program had also been terminated.

In Abiyot's mind, she heard two voices: one voice telling her to quit on life, and the other encouraging her to persevere. Fortunately, she listened to the second voice, the one that told her gently to count her blessings and to think positively about her future possibilities. The next day, she headed to the only place where she thought she could get help, a center founded by Compassion International, a Canadian organization dedicated to helping needy children. The Compassion center provided her family with money to buy food that day, as well as long-term assistance to cover the cost of groceries until their situation improved.

While Abiyot's story has a happy ending, there are, sadly, millions of such cases that do not. Researchers estimate that about 700 million people suffer each year from hunger and malnutrition. The continuing COVID-19 pandemic could add more than 130 million people into a situation of chronic hunger. Each day, about 25,000 people, including more than 10,000 children, die from hunger and related causes. The UN's goal of achieving "Zero Hunger by 2030" is now in grave doubt.

ISSUE 15 HUNGER AND MALNOURISHMENT

Vocabulary & Expressions:

dystopian
* referring to a place where people are unhappy, fearful, and treated unfairly
  - We use the word *dystopian* to describe a place where everything is as bad as it can be, and we use the word *utopian* to refer to a place where everything is as good as it can be.

to fight for existence
* to struggle to survive; to be in danger of dying
  - People who live in poor countries have *to fight for existence* every day.

despair
* the feeling of no longer having any hope or confidence
  - During difficult economic times, many people become hopeless and turn to *despair*.

abandon
* to leave and never return to someone who needs protection or help
  - The famous singer Adele was raised by her mother because her father *abandoned* the family when she was only three years old.

to add insult to injury
* to do or say something that makes a bad situation even worse for another person
  - Due to a bad economy, the company forced people to work longer hours, and *to add insult to injury*, the company decided not to give any pay raises.

laid off
* to lose your job, usually because of a bad economy or slow business
  - If the economy is bad, workers may be *laid off*; if workers don't do their jobs properly, they may be *fired*.

terminated
* to be ended, concluded
  - If you don't fulfill your duties in a business contract, the contract may be *terminated* by the other person.

persevere
* to keep trying to do something in spite of difficulties
  - Studying another language is difficult, and you need to *persevere* to learn it well.

count one's blessings
* to think carefully about the good things in one's life
  - When you think life is treating you badly, just stop and *count your blessings*; you will find many things to be thankful for.

cover the cost
* to pay for certain expenses
  - My car was damaged in an accident, but my insurance *covered the cost* to repair it.

malnutrition
* a condition of weakness and poor health that results from not eating enough food or from eating food that is not healthy
  - The Nobel Peace Prize was awarded in 2020 to the World Food Programme for its efforts to combat hunger and *malnutrition* around the world.

chronic
* continuing for a long time or returning often
  - Diabetes is a *chronic* disease, but it can be controlled with medicine and diet.

grave
* very serious; very important
  - The issue of drug addiction is a *grave* problem that many cities must face.

Open to Debate (2): 30 Global Issues

Open to Debate (2): 30 Global Issues

Discussion Points:

1. Do poor people in your country ever go hungry? How should your government solve this problem?
2. Have you ever donated money to help hungry people in other countries? Where did you donate the money?
3. Have you ever given money or food to a homeless person? What happened?
4. The United Nations World Food Programme says that $6.6 billion would solve the world's hunger problem. Why don't billionaires simply donate this amount?

Read the following quotes about world hunger.
Can you explain what they mean? Do you agree with the idea expressed?

5. There are people in the world so hungry, that God cannot appear to them except in the form of bread. Mahatma Gandhi
6. If we can conquer space, we can conquer childhood hunger.
   Buzz Aldrin, American astronaut who walked on the moon
7. If you cannot feed a hundred people, then feed just one. Mother Teresa

Current Hot Topic: Global Food Waste

While millions of Earth's residents go hungry every day, a shocking amount of food is wasted. About 25% of the world's food supply is lost each day. The world's population will reach more than nine billion by 2050, so the need to solve the problem of wasted food is urgent. France has tackled this problem with a very simple solution. A law has been passed that bans grocery stores from throwing away unsold food. If the food is still safe to eat, it must be donated to charity; if not, it must go to farmers for use as animal feed.

For Further Discussion:

1. What are the best ways to solve the problem of global food waste, in your opinion?
2. What happens to unused food in your country? Would you like to see your country pass a law like the one in France?

Issue 15 Hunger and Malnourishment

— Some people are scaling the fence! Aren't you going to arrest them?
— No, not at all.
— Why not? Aren't they illegal immigrants?
— Yeah, but if they succeed in scaling the fence, we'll give them citizenship. We've built the fence not because we want to block illegal immigrants but because we are testing them to see if they're strong and brave enough to scale the fence. They can join the US Army without training in boot camp. Don't you know our military forces have had difficulty recruiting new soldiers for a long time?
— How about the children? Isn't the fence too high for them to scale?
— Yes, it is. That's why we're considering lowering the fence ASAP.

The fence is too high for us! That's not fair! We thought the United States of America was a symbol of fairness in every aspect of life, including immigration. Please lower the fence at once!

Topic Preview:

Does your country have many foreign workers? What sort of jobs do they do? Is it easy for them to become citizens of your country? Would you support policies that allow more immigration?

Dialogue:

Lily: Adam, I'm curious about immigration policies in your home country of Australia.

Adam: Really? What do you want to know?

Lily: Well, do Australians welcome immigrants to their country?

Adam: I think that, in general, Australia is a very welcoming place. About 30% of Australians were born somewhere else.

Lily: I see. So politicians are usually pro-immigration?

Adam: Yes, they are, actually. All of the major political parties are pro-immigration.

Lily: Wow! That's quite a contrast with American political parties.

Adam: Yeah, I think you're right about that. By the way, would you like to immigrate to Australia?

Lily: Yeah, I'm thinking about it.

Adam: Well, you should do it. You would be welcomed with open arms.

Immigration

Mikhail Brin wanted a better future for his family. He worked as a mathematician and lived with his family in a three-bedroom apartment in central Moscow, but the family suffered discrimination because of their Jewish ethnicity. In 1977, he announced to his family that it was time for them to emigrate from Russia. A year later, he took the bold step of formally applying for an exit visa, and as a result he was promptly fired. His wife was also fired. For the next eight months, the family had no steady income, and they were forced to take temporary jobs as they waited to see what would become of their application to leave the country. In May 1979, they were granted their official exit visa.

The Brin family first lived in Vienna and Paris though their ultimate goal was to move to the United States. When Mikhail Brin managed to secure a position teaching mathematics at the University of Maryland, the family finally arrived in the US on October 25, 1979. Little Sergey Brin was only six years old, but he quickly acclimated to American life. He eventually graduated from the University of Maryland, with honors, in computer science and mathematics at the age of 19. Later, Brin attended Stanford University, where he met Larry Page. The two worked together to create an Internet search engine called BackRub, which eventually morphed into Google. Both men are multibillionaires now.

Of course, not every story of immigration creates a new billionaire. However, many immigrants end up bettering the lives of their families. According to the Universal Declaration of Human Rights, people have the right to leave their home country if they choose. Article 13 states, "Everyone has the right to leave any country, including his own, and to return to his country."

ISSUE 16 IMMIGRATION

Vocabulary & Expressions:

ethnicity
*relating to races or large groups of people who have the same customs, religion, origin, or similar characteristics
- Al Pacino's grandparents came from Italy, so his *ethnicity* is Italian.

emigrate from
*to leave one's country to live elsewhere; not to be confused with *immigrate to*
- Many Irish people *emigrated from* Ireland in the 19th century; many of them *immigrated* to the US.

exit visa
*a document that lets a person leave a country
- Countries that require US citizens to have *exit visas* include Russia, Belarus, Saudi Arabia, and Qatar.

steady
*continuing for a long period of time in a dependable way
- If you are a doctor or nurse, you will always have a job and a *steady* income.

become of
*to happen to
- I have lost touch with all of my high school friends; I always wonder what *became of* them.

manage to
*to succeed in doing something; to accomplish what is desired
- My sister is so smart; she *managed to* graduate from college in three years.

secure
*to get hold of, acquire
- Most college graduates want to *secure* a job as soon as they finish their college education.

position
*a place of employment; a job
- After my sister graduated from college, she got a *position* at Samsung.

acclimate to
*to adjust or change to fit a new climate or situation
- My father worked in Kuwait for a while, but he had trouble *acclimating* to the hot weather.

with honors
*a special rank or distinction given by a university to a student who did extremely well in academics
- Jodie Foster graduated *with honors* from Yale University, where she got a literature degree.

morph
*to gradually change into a different thing; to be transformed
- Amazon.com was founded in 1994 to sell books, but it eventually *morphed* into the world's largest retailer of all kinds of products.

better
*to make or become more satisfactory
- Most cities do their best to *better* the lives of the homeless.

Universal Declaration of Human Rights
*an international document adopted in 1948 by the United Nations General Assembly that lists the rights and freedoms that all human beings should have
- Article 17 of the *Universal Declaration of Human Rights* states that every person has the right to own property.

Discussion Points:

1. What are the advantages of immigrating to another country? What are the disadvantages?
2. Can you think of any immigrants who have become successful in your country? What happened?
3. Do you know anyone who has immigrated to another country? What is their life like there?
4. Would you like to see more immigrants or fewer immigrants coming to your country?
5. Have you ever dreamed about moving to another country to start a new life? Which country would you choose?

Read the following quotes about immigration.
Can you explain what they mean? Do you agree with the idea expressed?

6. One of the reasons why Canadians are generally positively inclined towards immigration is we've seen over decades, over generations, that it works. Justin Trudeau
7. My fellow Americans, we are and always will be a nation of immigrants. We were strangers once, too. Barack Obama

Current Hot Topic: Anti-Immigration Politics

Despite the benefits of immigration, some countries, especially in Europe, are now adopting anti-immigration policies. In France, politician Marine Le Pen has been accused of supporting racist, anti-Muslim, anti-immigrant policies. She is opposed to globalization and believes that multiculturalism has failed. In spite of these policies, she received 34% of the vote in the 2017 presidential election, running against Emmanuel Macron. Anti-immigrant sentiment is highest in Hungary, where about two-thirds of the people are opposed to immigration. Anti-immigration politicians have won victories in Austria, Poland, the Czech Republic, and Slovenia. Even in Sweden, anti-immigration policies have become more popular.

For Further Discussion:

1. Why do you think so many Europeans are opposed to immigration? What are their primary fears?
2. Does your government support policies that are favorable to immigration? Have you heard any politicians give anti-immigration speeches?

I don't smoke, drink, and do drugs, but I can't escape from Internet addiction.

I'm surprised that "friendship" can be formed so easily online thanks to the revolutionary Internet.

I didn't know the Internet is the most powerful magnet in the world. Anyone who has a smartphone is bewitched by it.

I'm afraid of becoming too fascinated by the Internet. That's why I'm still using a "stupid" phone instead of a smartphone.

Topic Preview:

Do you know anyone who spends too much time on the Internet? What do they do while they're on the Internet? What is the greatest number of hours that you have spent using the Internet in a single day? What are your three most common reasons for getting on the Internet?

Dialogue:

Kimberly: Donald, I don't know what I'm going to do about my little brother!

Donald: What are you talking about?

Kimberly: He's only 15, and he seems to be addicted to computer games. He must be online for five hours or more every day.

Donald: Wow! That does seem like a lot. How can he possibly find time to do his homework?

Kimberly: Well, sometimes he just doesn't get it finished. At other times, he finishes it, but it's poorly done.

Donald: Aren't your parents concerned about his behavior?

Kimberly: Of course, they are, but they aren't sure what to do.

Donald: Hmmm… if he continues this addictive behavior, maybe you should put him in one of those "Internet detox" programs.

Kimberly: I think you're right. We may have to do that very soon, or his addiction could get worse.

Donald: I know some programs that could help. I'll send you the links.

Kimberly: Okay. Thanks.

Internet Addiction

Rustam was a 17-year-old Russian teen who loved playing computer games. It seemed almost like a blessing when he broke his leg and was confined to his home because it meant that he could play his favorite game, *Defense of the Ancients*, continuously. He became fixated on playing the game, and over a period of 22 days, he played continuously, stopping only to take a nap and grab a snack. One day, all went quiet in his room. When his parents went into his room to check on him, he had collapsed, ironically, at the same time as his online persona was also killed in the game. He was rushed to the hospital, but he was declared dead on arrival. Doctors believe that he died from a thrombosis, a condition that happens sometimes to someone who sits continuously for a long time, such as a passenger on a cramped long-haul flight.

The tragic case of this game-obsessed teenager is just one of many such incidents. In China, a 22-year-old man was rushed to the hospital after playing online games for four days in a row, without eating or drinking, and coming down with a kidney disorder. In South Korea, another man in his 20s died after playing online games for 86 hours without sleep. Another 20-something Korean man was charged with murdering his mother because she nagged him about wasting too much time playing games.

Addiction to online games has become so widespread that the ICD has added an entry to its list of diseases, namely, "gaming disorder." This disorder describes a pattern of gaming behavior that results in significant impairment in personal, family, social, educational, occupational, or other important areas of functioning. Many countries have created detox centers, where people try to free themselves from their addictive behavior.

ISSUE 17 INTERNET ADDICTION

Vocabulary & Expressions:

confined
*unable to leave a place because of illness, imprisonment, or a similar reason
- When my brother got the COVID-19 virus, he was *confined* to his house for ten days.

fixated
*having an obsessive attachment to someone or something
- My cousin is *fixated* on sports; he watches sports on TV every day.

ironically
*happening in a strange or funny way because a situation is different from what you expected
- *Ironically*, the driver crashed his car into the police station.

persona
*an identity or character that a person chooses to represent himself or herself
- In computing, an avatar is a visual representation of a user's character or *persona*.

dead on arrival
*having died before arriving at a hospital; abbreviated as DOA
- There was a terrible car accident near my house; sadly, the victim was *dead on arrival* at the hospital.

thrombosis
*a serious medical condition caused when a blood clot blocks the flow of blood in a blood vessel
- Passengers on long airplane flights need to get up and walk around sometimes on the plane in order to avoid *thrombosis*.

cramped
*confined or severely limited in space
- My tiny apartment has very *cramped* closets.

long-haul
*relating to a long journey or distance
- When I visited Singapore, I took the *long-haul* flight from New York to Singapore, which took almost 18 hours.

ICD
*_The International Classification of Diseases_, a book or database that lists and classifies every disease
- The *ICD* is published by the World Health Organization and is used around the world to identify diseases.

impairment
*a condition in which part of your body, mind, or social life is weakened or damaged and does not work well
- My grandfather lived to be 102, but he suffered some mental *impairment* in his last year of life.

detox
*an abbreviation for *detoxification*, which refers to the process of helping someone to stop using drugs, alcohol, or some addictive behavior
- Many countries have formed *detox* centers to help young people break their addiction to computer games.

free
*to cause someone to stop being affected by something unpleasant, painful, or unwanted
- My father smoked for ten years, but he was eventually able to *free* himself from that bad habit.

Open to Debate (2): 30 Global Issues

Discussion Points:

1. Have you heard about any tragic stories about gaming addiction in your country? What happened?
2. Why is playing computer games so addictive?
3. Do you know anyone who spends an excessive amount of time playing computer games? What is their life like?
4. Does your country have any programs to help gaming addicts to break their bad habits? Do you know anyone who participated in such a program?
5. How many hours do you spend each week playing computer games? How many hours do you spend on social media? How about using your smartphone?

Read the following quotes about technology addiction.
Can you explain what they mean? Do you agree with the idea expressed?

6. The difference between technology and slavery is that slaves are fully aware that they are not free. Nassim Nicholas Taleb
7. People love video games because they do things they obviously can't do in real life. Ralph H. Baer

Current Hot Topic: The Causes of Internet Addiction

There is not universal agreement as to what causes Internet addiction and gaming disorder. However, it is known that boys aged 8 to 17 are the most vulnerable. The causes that contribute to an individual becoming addicted to computer games or the Internet include the following: poor mental health, poor impulse control, anxiety, depression, and social isolation. Thus, addicts typically have poor emotional, physical, mental, and social health. Warning signs of a possible gaming addiction include the following: new problems while at school, a decline in social interaction with family and friends, and a loss of interest in previous hobbies.

For Further Discussion:

1. What is the best aspect of having the Internet? What is the worst aspect?
2. Have you ever felt that you were spending too much time on the Internet? What did you do to change your behavior?

Topic Preview:

Does your country's government censor the Internet? In what ways? Is Internet censorship ever acceptable? In what situations? Do parents in your country use software to control what their children can access on the Internet? Is this approach a good idea?

Dialogue:

Karen: Anthony, I wonder if you can help me with an Internet issue. I want to download some videos for educational purposes, but I don't want to get into trouble for violation of copyright.

Anthony: Do you know how to download materials using bit torrents?

Karen: Yes, I do, but companies can still see your IP and complain to your Internet service provider that you are downloading copyright material.

Anthony: Yes, that's true, and those companies will probably not accept your explanation that you are downloading material for educational purposes and not for resale.

Karen: Exactly! Do you have any ideas of how I can get around that problem?

Anthony: Yes, of course. You need to get a VPN or "virtual private network."

Karen: Hmmm… how does that work?

Anthony: A VPN provides you with an anonymous IP, so no company can complain to your Internet service provider. You can use the Internet without censorship.

Karen: I see. Well, can you show me how to set up a VPN?

Anthony: Yes, of course—for a small fee.

Karen: What? Are you going to charge me?

Anthony: I was just kidding! I'll be happy to help you. It's easy to do.

Internet Censorship

Alexander Lukashenko, the president of Belarus, proudly refers to himself as "Europe's last dictator." Many Belarusians hoped that the national election in 2020 would lead to the end of his brutal, authoritarian rule. Unfortunately, they were sorely disappointed. The government announced that Lukashenko was reelected with 80% of the vote. International monitors claimed that the elections were not free and fair, leading to sanctions on Lukashenko and others. His disputed victory led to widespread allegations of vote rigging and massive anti-government protests. The Belarusian government responded with a vicious crackdown on demonstrators and by disrupting Internet access and restricting online content. This extensive Internet censorship continues to this day.

When the COVID-19 outbreak occurred in the city of Wuhan, China, in February 2020, a local lawyer-turned-journalist named Zhang Zhan took it on herself to report what was happening. She began to use live-streaming video reports on social media that showed the city's hospitals, families, and streets. Her reporting was one of the most valuable sources of independent information about the health situation in Wuhan. However, her online postings began to disappear due to censorship by the Chinese government. She was later arrested and sentenced to four years' imprisonment based on the nebulous charge of "picking quarrels and provoking trouble." Meanwhile, Reporters without Borders (RWB) awarded her its 2021 Prize for Courage in appreciation of her honest journalism.

It would be a mistake to conclude that Internet censorship only occurs in nondemocratic countries. The RWB maintains a list of "Enemies of the Internet," which includes the countries that practice various forms of censorship in order to control people's access to information. Included on the list are prominent democratic countries, including the UK and the US. Another list includes countries "under surveillance" for their censorship activities, including Australia, France, and South Korea.

ISSUE 18 INTERNET CENSORSHIP

Vocabulary & Expressions:

brutal   *cruel and harsh
- During wartime, armies on both sides usually commit many *brutal* acts.

authoritarian   *requiring people to obey strict rules or laws; not allowing personal freedom
- For some countries, it can take many years to move from an *authoritarian* government to a democratic one.

sorely   *extremely, very
- I was *sorely* tempted to argue with my angry boss.

sanctions   *actions taken by one or more nations to make another nation and its rulers comply with a law or rule
- In the early 1990s, the United Nations imposed many *sanctions* on Iraq because it invaded Kuwait.

dispute   *to question or deny the truthfulness or rightness of a claim or situation
- The result of the US presidential election in 2000 was *disputed* at first, but the issue was resolved with a decision by the Supreme Court.

rig   *to control the result of an election by deceptive or dishonest means
- Some Americans claimed without evidence that the US presidential election in 2020 was *rigged* in favor of Joe Biden.

vicious   *very violent, cruel, and dangerous
- Criminals who commit *vicious* crimes should receive a very long prison sentence.

crackdown   *an increased effort to enforce a law or rule
- Recently, the police began a *crackdown* on unlicensed street vendors in my city.

disrupt   *to stop the normal progress or activity of something
- Last night several dogs barked loudly and *disrupted* my sleep.

take it on oneself   *to do something that needs to be done even though no one has asked you to do it
- Once I heard that the teacher's birthday was next Friday, I *took it on myself* to collect money from the students for a small birthday gift.

nebulous   *not clear or specific, vague
- The teacher's instructions about the homework were *nebulous*; students were not sure what they were required to do.

nondemocratic   *not following the principles or practice of democracy, where supreme power is held by the citizens
- The OECD supports democratic governments and economic policies, so *nondemocratic* governments are not allowed to join.

surveillance   *the act of carefully watching someone or something, especially in order to detect a crime or violation of human rights
- The FBI frequently keeps suspected criminals under *surveillance* for months before they are arrested for their crimes.

Open to Debate (2): 30 Global Issues

Discussion Points:

1. What examples of government censorship of the Internet have you heard about? What happened?
2. Is there any country that has absolutely no Internet censorship? Would you like to live there?
3. What types of Internet censorship can you name that are actually valid (e.g., protecting children from pornographic sites, blocking illegal gambling sites)?
4. Did your parents ever monitor your use of the Internet through software, such as Net Nanny?

Read the following quotes about Internet censorship.
Can you explain what they mean? Do you agree with the idea expressed?

5. When you have strict censorship of the Internet, young students cannot receive a full education. Their view of the world is imbalanced. There can be no true discussion of the issues. Ai Weiwei
6. There is a fine line between censorship and good taste and moral responsibility. Steven Spielberg
7. The only valid censorship of ideas is the right of people not to listen. Tom Smothers

Current Hot Topic: Encrypted Email Accounts

Switzerland is a famous haven for Internet freedom and privacy. Strict federal laws guarantee the protection of personal data and a lack of censorship. ProtonMail chose the country as its base for launching an end-to-end encrypted email service in 2013. ProtonMail boasts that they don't have the technical ability to decrypt user messages, and as a result, it is impossible for them to hand over user data to law enforcement. In spite of this bold claim, in 2021, ProtonMail was forced by a Swiss court order to hand over the IP addresses of French activists who were charged with crimes.

For Further Discussion:

1. If ProtonMail can be forced to hand over users' IP addresses, can there truly be an encrypted email account that cannot be accessed by law enforcement?
2. What email service do you use? Could your government successfully access the content with a court order?

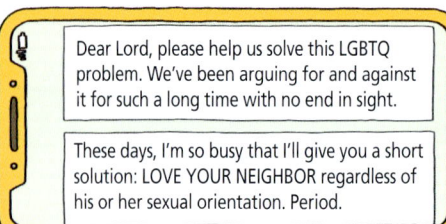

Topic Preview:

Who are the most famous gay people in your country? What is life like for them? Do you have any friends who are gay? Do you have any religious friends who think that being gay is a sin?

Dialogue:

Carol: Hey, David. I need your help. I'm writing a research paper about LGBTQ celebrities. Can you think of any?

David: Of course. The first one who comes to mind is Lady Gaga.

Carol: She's gay? I had no idea.

David: Well, actually, she identifies as bisexual, not gay.

Carol: I see. Can you think of any others?

David: Jodie Foster, Kristen Stewart, and Ellen Page.

Carol: Wow! You are a great source of information! What about men who are gay?

David: Of course, there's Elton John. I can also think of Anderson Cooper, Lance Bass, and Ricky Martin.

Carol: How do you know so much about gay celebrities?

David: I read a lot of entertainment magazines.

LGBTQ

Amir grew up in Iran. At age 13, he realized that he was gay, and he even found a boyfriend. In spite of warnings from their religious teacher, the two boys continued their relationship. Eventually, school authorities took Amir, beat him, and tortured him by pulling his fingers out of joint. Then Amir and his friend were both expelled from school. The friend's parents moved out of Tehran, and Amir never saw him again. Sometime later, Amir was arrested by the religious police on his way home. They punished him with 90 lashes. The pain was so severe that he cried out for his mother. He couldn't sleep on his back for months.

Despite the beatings, Amir could not change who he was. He found a new relationship with a man but was caught and put in jail. He was sure that he would be executed. However, his father paid a bribe and got him out. After Amir got home, his mother gave him a counterfeit passport and money to leave the country. He eventually made his way to London, where he lives today as an undocumented worker. He is reluctant to apply for asylum because he is afraid that the authorities will repatriate him to Iran.

As Amir's story demonstrates, life is difficult in certain countries for anyone whose sexual orientation falls within the category of LGBTQ. This initialism refers to individuals who are lesbian, gay, bisexual, transgender, or questioning. Being gay is considered a psychological disease in Iran and is punishable by death. In fact, being gay is illegal in more than 70 countries, including Egypt, Libya, Sudan, Gambia, and Nigeria. At the other end of the spectrum there are countries like Sweden, France, Belgium, Canada, and New Zealand, where you are accepted for who you are.

ISSUE 19 LGBTQ

Vocabulary & Expressions:

torture   *the act of causing great pain, especially to punish someone
- In most countries, it is against the law for the police to *torture* a criminal suspect.

expel   *to force someone to leave a school or other organization
- If a student brings a knife to school, he will probably be *expelled*.

religious police   *a police force that enforces religious laws and public morality
- The *religious police* in Malaysia monitor people to make sure they follow strict Islamic laws, such as not drinking alcohol.

lashes   *blows on a person's body with a whip or switch
- In times of slavery, slaves could be given many *lashes* if they disobeyed their owners.

counterfeit   *something that is made to look like an exact copy of something else in order to trick people
- Making *counterfeit* money or IDs is a serious crime punishable by many years in prison.

make one's way   *to go in a particular direction or to a particular destination
- After dropping out of college in the 1960s, Harrison Ford *made his way* to Hollywood, where he eventually became a superstar.

undocumented   *not having the official documents that are needed to enter, live in, or work in a country legally
- If *undocumented* workers are found by police, they are usually sent back to their home country.

asylum   *protection given by a government to someone who has left another country because they might be harmed there
- Many people who are persecuted because of their race or religion come to the US and apply for *asylum*.

repatriate   *to return someone to his or her own country
- If you are caught working in a foreign country without the proper documents, you will be *repatriated*.

sexual orientation   *a person's sexual identity as straight, gay, or bisexual
- Most modern people now believe that a person's *sexual orientation* is not their choice, so they avoid the biased term *sexual preference*.

initialism   *an abbreviation formed from initial letters of a name or organization, such as *FBI* for Federal Bureau of Investigation
- Some people use the word *initialism* to refer to abbreviations where each letter is pronounced separately, as in *FBI*, and the word *acronym* to refer to abbreviations that are pronounced as words, as in *NASA*; however, other people use *initialism* and *acronym* interchangeably.

spectrum   *a complete range of different opinions, people, moods, and so forth
- There is a broad *spectrum* of political beliefs in most countries, ranging from very liberal to very conservative.

Open to Debate (2): 30 Global Issues

Open to Debate (2): 30 Global Issues

Discussion Points:

1. Do gay people in your country have the same legal rights as straight people?
2. Would a gay teacher be allowed in your country? Have you ever had one?
3. Do you think that gay people should be allowed to serve in the military? Why or why not?
4. If your child announced that he or she were gay, how would you respond?

Read the following quotes about LGBTQ rights.
Can you explain what they mean? Do you agree with the idea expressed?

5. Gay rights are human rights; there is no separation. Macklemore
6. Being gay is like being left-handed. Some people are, most people aren't, and nobody really knows why. It's not right or wrong; it's just the way things are. Unknown
7. Nature made a mistake, which I have corrected. Christine Jorgensen [One of the first people to undergo sex change surgery, or "sex reassignment surgery"]

Current Hot Topic: Transgender Athletes

Should transgender athletes be allowed to compete in sports? The International Olympic Committee says yes. While the IOC has allowed transgender athletes to participate at the Olympics since 2004, no transgender athletes had taken advantage of that provision until the 2020 Summer Olympics, which were actually held in Tokyo in 2021. Laurel Hubbard, a trans woman from New Zealand competed in weightlifting, although she won no medals. Soccer player Quinn helped the Canadian team win the gold medal. Alana Smith represented the US in the women's skateboarding semifinals. Meanwhile, in the US, some states have banned trans athletes from competing.

For Further Discussion:

1. Do you think transgender athletes should be allowed to compete against traditional athletes? What are the pros and cons?
2. How are transgender people accepted in your country? Do they have the same freedoms as everyone else?

Topic Preview:

What is the life expectancy for people in your country? Is it the same for men and women? How old would you like to live to? How old do you think you will live to?

Dialogue:

Jennifer: Hey, Daniel. What are you doing this weekend?

Daniel: Oh, I'm going to a special birthday party.

Jennifer: Who's having a birthday—a friend of yours?

Daniel: Not exactly. My grandmother will be turning 100 years old on Saturday.

Jennifer: Wow! That's amazing! That really is a special event.

Daniel: Yeah, all her children, grandchildren, and great-grandchildren will be there.

Jennifer: That's awesome. By the way, has your grandmother ever revealed her secret to living such a long time?

Daniel: She has, actually. She says you should eat lots of fruits and vegetables and don't consume too much alcohol and red meat.

Jennifer: Well, that sounds reasonable.

Daniel: Yes, it does. I'm going to do my best to follow her advice.

Jennifer: Okay. Well, have a good time at the birthday party.

Life Expectancy

The Central African Republic has an abundance of natural resources, but it remains one of the poorest nations on planet Earth. This landlocked country has a population of less than five million people, but 90% of them live in poverty, with little access to food, suitable housing, water, or sanitation. To make matters worse, various civil wars have decimated the country in recent years. Over 600,000 displaced people live in churches, mosques, and public buildings. Many of them are forced to sleep in the open, making them vulnerable to inclement weather conditions.

Thousands of Central Africans have entered neighboring Cameroon, where their lives are marginally better. Nearly half of them are under the age of 14 years, and many of these children have been orphaned by AIDS or civil war. With this background, it is not surprising to discover that the life expectancy of Central Africans is only about 53 years, making it one of the shortest life expectancies in the world.

About 12,000 km away from the Central African Republic lies Japan, an island nation of over 125 million people. The Japanese government guarantees high-quality health care for everyone, and the country has one of the best health care systems in the world. The country has the third highest GDP in the world and is a global leader in the automotive and electronics industries. It comes as no surprise then to learn that the Japanese life expectancy is more than 84 years of age, the highest in the world. Japan probably has more living centenarians today than any other country. Japan is also the home country of the verified oldest man in history, Jiroemon Kimura, who lived from April 19, 1897, to June 12, 2013, a total of 116 years and 54 days.

ISSUE 20 LIFE EXPECTANCY

Vocabulary & Expressions:

natural resources *something, such as water, minerals, forests, or animals, that is found in nature and is valuable to humans
- The most important *natural resources* in South Korea are its forests and various mineral resources, such as graphite, iron ore, coal, and zinc.

landlocked *enclosed or nearly enclosed by land
- Kazakhstan is the largest *landlocked* country in the world; it has no access to an ocean or sea.

decimate *to destroy a large amount or number of something
- The insects *decimated* the farmer's corn.

displaced *when people or animals are forced to leave the area where they live
- Many thousands of people have been *displaced* by the war in Syria.

mosque *a building used for public worship by Muslims
- Christians worship God in a church, but Muslims worship in a *mosque*.

vulnerable *capable of being easily hurt or injured
- Older people are often more *vulnerable* to disease.

inclement *having rain, storms, or other types of severe weather
- Florida has very sunny weather, but it can also have *inclement* weather, such as hurricanes.

marginally *slightly, a little, somewhat; on a small scale
- The sales of new cars were *marginally* better this year compared to last year.

orphan *to cause a child to have no parents
- One of the terrible results of war is that many children are *orphaned*.

GDP *gross domestic product, the total amount of the market value of all the goods and services produced in a country for a certain period
- The US has the largest *GDP* in the world, followed by China, Japan, Germany, and the UK.

centenarian *a person who is at least 100 years old
- If you reach age 100, you are a *centenarian*; if you reach age 110, you are a *supercentenarian*.

verified *confirmed as being accurate or correct by acceptable evidence
- The oldest *verified* age to which any human has ever lived is 122 years and 164 days, by Jeanne Calment (1875–1997) of France.

Open to Debate (2): 30 Global Issues

Discussion Points:

1. Nine out of the ten countries with the lowest life expectancy are in Africa. Why do you think this is true?
2. Would you be willing for your country to contribute more foreign aid to help poor countries?
3. Why do you think Japanese people have such a long life expectancy?
4. What are the advantages to living a long time? What are the disadvantages?

Read the following quotes about living a long life.
Can you explain what they mean? Do you agree with the idea expressed?

5. Age isn't a number; it's an attitude. Unknown
6. It is better to have a meaningful life and make a difference than to merely have a long life. Bryant H. McGill
7. Our days may come to seventy years,
   or eighty, if our strength endures;
   yet the best of them are but trouble and sorrow,
   for they quickly pass, and we fly away. Psalm 90:10

Current Hot Topic: Keys to Living a Long Life

Italian scientists claim to have found the secrets to a long life. They conducted their research in the small village of Acciaroli, Italy, where one in ten residents lives to be 100 years old. Even in old age, the residents have low levels of dementia, heart disease, and other chronic conditions associated with old age. A local centenarian, Antonio Vassalo, explains, "We only eat healthy stuff. We eat a lot of fish, fresh produce, olive oil, and local products." Scientists agree that this Mediterranean diet, along with a moderate consumption of protein and lots of walking, offers many health benefits.

For Further Discussion:

1. In your view, what are the best habits you should have for living a long time? What are the worst habits that can shorten your life expectancy?
2. Who has lived the longest in your family? Why do you think they lived such a long time?

— Dad, what can we do? Everything is gone, including our house. But this one building survived the hurricane intact! How can it be?

— It's the state penitentiary, Son. They've built it so strong that prisoners cannot escape.

— Life isn't fair! Good things happen to bad people while bad things happen to good people like us. How can I enter this strong building? What crimes should I commit?

I was wrongfully convicted, but I think it was God's plan to save me. I'll give up appealing my case and stay here until doomsday.

Our prison is getting very crowded as the hurricane season is nearing. I think we have just two choices: release all the prisoners, except for the worst criminals, or make all the prisoners pay fees for their own support.

I was lucky that I was charged with murder, so I could stay here safely amid such a severe hurricane. I can eat three meals, read books, watch TV, and exercise free of charge. But I'm so upset that I'm supposed to be released next month. Now I'm thinking that I should commit another crime outside, so I will be locked up here once again.

Topic Preview:

What are the most common types of natural disasters in your country? Have you ever experienced one? What happened? Does your country's government do a good job of warning citizens about coming natural disasters?

Dialogue:

Emily: Hey, Charles. I know you're from Miami. Have you ever experienced a hurricane?

Charles: Yes, I have, actually—quite a few.

Emily: What was the worst one that you remember?

Charles: Oh, that would be Hurricane Irma, which struck in September 2017.

Emily: What made it so bad?

Charles: It had winds of over 200 kmh, and it caused electricity to go out for more than seven million people.

Emily: Wow! That's terrible!

Charles: Yeah, and it killed 84 people and did $50 billion in damage.

Emily: Oh my! That's awful.

Charles: Yeah, it was pretty bad. Fortunately, my family lived far inland, so we were not hurt.

Natural Disasters

Tom and Arlette Stuip of the Netherlands were vacationing in Khao Lak, Thailand, on a Boxing Day some years ago. Early in the day, they felt the ground tremble from an earthquake. Later, the couple was eating breakfast when they noticed that the servers were all pointing at the sea, which was receding rapidly, leaving the bare seabed. Tourists on the beach began to take out their cameras and walk toward the exposed seabed. However, Tom knew that something was wrong. Then he remembered the earthquake that had occurred earlier.

It became clear to Tom that the retreating water was the prelude to a tidal wave. Tom grabbed Arlette's hand and yelled, "Run!" At that moment, they saw a wall of water, 6–10 m in height, rushing toward them at a speed of 60–80 kmh. They ran uphill as fast as they could, with the deafening surge of water right behind them. As it turned out, they survived the 2004 Indian Ocean Tsunami (AKA the Boxing Day Tsunami). More than 227,000 people in 14 countries died that day, making it one of the deadliest natural disasters in recorded history.

María Belón, a Spanish physician, was also on vacation in Thailand with her husband and three sons. She was severely injured and nearly died in the tsunami. Years later, a film entitled *The Impossible* (2012) was based on the true story of how María and her family survived. Nowadays, María travels the world as a motivational speaker. She describes her experience as follows: "The tsunami was an incredible gift. I embrace life. My whole life is extra time. I do not deserve to be alive, but life is not fair. I feel pain and compassion for so many others who didn't come back up or lost the ones they love."

ISSUE 21 NATURAL DISASTERS

Vocabulary & Expressions:

Boxing Day
* a holiday celebrated on December 26th, especially in Great Britain and its former colonies
  - *Boxing Day* originated as a holiday to give gifts to the poor, but nowadays it's primarily known as a shopping holiday.

tremble
* to shake or vibrate because of some force
  - The shoppers felt the building *tremble*; later, they found out that an earthquake had occurred.

recede
* to move back or away
  - After the rain stopped, the floodwaters began to *recede*.

retreat
* to move back or away
  - Scientists are concerned that glaciers are *retreating* because of global warming.

prelude
* a preliminary event that comes before and leads to an action, event, or situation of higher importance
  - My boss's negative evaluation during my annual job review was a *prelude* to his firing of me a month later.

tidal wave
* a very high sea wave that sometimes follows an earthquake; a tsunami
  - The largest *tidal wave* in history occurred on July 10, 1958, when an earthquake in Alaska caused waves that were 520 meters high.

surge
* a large wave
  - Surfers like to ride their surfboards on a huge *surge* of water, as long as it's not too high.

as it turned out
* as it happened, often surprisingly or unexpectedly
  - I was worried when I asked Sonja for a date, but *as it turned out*, she said yes, and we had a good time.

AKA
* also known as
  - The Republic of Korea, *AKA* South Korea, has the 10th largest GDP in the world, according to the World Bank.

recorded history
* a historical narrative based on written records or documents
  - *Recorded history* begins with the invention of writing and the existence of written accounts of the ancient world, around the 4th millennium BC.

motivational speaker
* a person who makes speeches intended to inspire, challenge, or motivate an audience
  - Nick Vujicic was born without arms or legs; he learned to live with his condition and became a famous *motivational speaker*.

Open to Debate (2): 30 Global Issues

Discussion Points:

1. Do you agree with religious people who say that natural disasters always have some purpose? If not, then why do they occur?
2. What is the worst natural disaster that your country has experienced recently? What happened?
3. Are some natural disasters actually caused in part by human beings? Can you cite some examples?
4. Have you ever personally experienced an earthquake? What happened?

Read the following quotes about natural disasters.
Can you explain what they mean? Do you agree with the idea expressed?

5. Even with all our technology and the inventions that make modern life so much easier than it once was, it takes just one big natural disaster to wipe all that away and remind us that, here on Earth, we're still at the mercy of nature. Neil deGrasse Tyson
6. In all natural disasters, man needs to attach meaning to tragedy, no matter how random and inexplicable the event is. Nathaniel Philbrick
7. We cannot stop natural disasters, but we can arm ourselves with knowledge; so many lives wouldn't have to be lost if there was enough disaster preparedness. Petra Němcová

Current Hot Topic: Natural Disasters and Nuclear Power

On March 11, 2011, the most powerful earthquake ever recorded in Japan occurred in the Pacific Ocean 72 km east of the Tōhoku region of Japan. It lasted six minutes, causing a massive tsunami that killed almost 20,000 people. The tsunami also caused the Fukushima Daiichi nuclear disaster, which released radioactive water into the Pacific Ocean and exposed thousands of local residents to harmful radiation. As a result of this disaster, many people demanded that nuclear power plants must never be built in areas that are subject to earthquakes. Others called for a complete elimination of nuclear power altogether.

For Further Discussion:

1. How much of your country's electrical power comes from nuclear power? Are any nuclear power plants built in areas that are subject to earthquakes and tsunamis?
2. Do you think nuclear power is safe? If not, would you support phasing out all nuclear power?

● **Topic Preview:**

Have you ever gone on a diet? Was your diet successful? Do you have any friends who are obese? Have you ever encouraged them to lose weight? What country do you think has the most obese people?

● **Dialogue:**

Dorothy: Hey, Thomas. Did you make any New Year's resolutions?

Thomas: Yes, I did, but I only made two resolutions.

Dorothy: Well, if you don't mind me asking, what were your resolutions?

Thomas: Number one: save more money.

Dorothy: Okay. That's a good one. I made that resolution too.

Thomas: Number two: lose three kilograms.

Dorothy: Oh, I'm surprised. Your weight looks normal to me.

Thomas: Well, I'm about three kilos over my ideal weight, so I'd like to lose it. I don't want to become obese.

Dorothy: Okay. I understand. Well, how do you plan to lose the weight?

Thomas: Cut out all desserts, and take a brisk, 30-minute walk every day.

Dorothy: That sounds like a good plan! Good luck!

Thomas: Thanks.

Obesity

It is ironic that millions of people are starving in poor and war-torn countries, while in other parts of the world, obesity continues at epidemic proportions. A British woman named Claire has been obese for her entire life. It all started when she was a child. Her mother would fill her plate with huge portion sizes and tell her, "Be sure to clean your plate! People in Africa are starving." On one occasion, when she did not eat every morsel on her plate, she was severely punished. She was dragged screaming across the room and locked into a garden shed, denied any dessert, and isolated from her family. She was only three years old at the time. Throughout her childhood, she was taught to consume huge portions of food, even if she felt so full that she was sick. Now she is 43 years old and weighs 178 kg.

Most people are aware that the United States is home to many obese people. Indeed, the most obese person who ever lived was an American man, Jon Brower Minnoch (1941–1983), who weighed 635 kg at his peak weight. However, the US is not the most obese country in the world. Almost all of the top ten obese countries are island nations in the Pacific Ocean. In Samoa, for example, most of the politicians and religious leaders are obese. Since church ministers are treated like traditional chiefs of Samoa, they are well fed by their followers. They also do not generally engage in any sports, which would be regarded as undignified by the local culture. Because most of the elites in the society are obese, people subconsciously make a positive correlation of power and influence with obesity. Thus, culture plays a major role in the prevalence of obesity in these nations.

ISSUE 22 OBESITY

Vocabulary & Expressions:

war-torn *very badly harmed or damaged by war
- South Korea was a ***war-torn*** country in the 1950s; nowadays, it is an economic powerhouse.

epidemic *describing something harmful that spreads or develops rapidly
- Some large cities are experiencing an ***epidemic*** crime wave.

proportions *the size, shape, or extent of something
- The government's economic failures created a crisis of great ***proportions***.

morsel *a small piece of food
- I used to give my dog ***morsels*** from the dinner table.

shed *a small building used especially for storage
- My dad always kept his tools in a ***shed*** behind our house.

chief *the ruler or head of a tribe or clan
- Every Native American tribe was headed by a powerful ***chief***.

undignified *lacking proper seriousness in behavior or appearance
- It is very ***undignified*** for teachers to use bad language.

elites *the people who have the most wealth, status, and power in a society
- Expensive parties are usually attended only by the ***elites*** of the city.

subconsciously *in a manner indicating that a person is not aware of something and does not consciously know or feel it
- Children who are often criticized by their parents grow up ***subconsciously*** feeling that they cannot do anything right.

positive correlation *a mutual relationship, such as cause and effect, of two or more things, parts, actions, or effects
- Researchers find a ***positive correlation*** between obesity and a lack of exercise.

play a major role *to be involved in; to be an important factor in
- Alcohol ***plays a major role*** in many car accidents.

prevalence *the condition of being widespread or generally true
- The bad economy has created the ***prevalence*** of pessimism among local people.

Open to Debate (2): 30 Global Issues

● ● ● ● Open to Debate (2): **30 Global Issues**

● **Discussion Points:**

1. Is rising obesity a problem in your country? If so, why do you think it's happening?
2. Did your parents ever say to you, "Clean your plate" or "People in Africa are starving"?
3. Do you know anyone who is overweight? What is this person's life like?
4. Are you satisfied with your current weight? If not, how much weight would you like to lose?

Read the following quotes about obesity.
Can you explain what they mean? Do you agree with the idea expressed?

5. You are what you eat. Victor Lindlahr
6. If losing weight was easy, we would all be skinny. Steven Magee
7. Obesity affects every aspect of a person's life, from health to relationships. Jane Velez-Mitchell
8. Child hunger and child obesity are really just two sides of the same coin. Both rob our children of the energy, the strength, and the stamina they need to succeed in school and in life. Michelle Obama

● **Current Hot Topic:** **Government Bans of Junk Food**

Should the government limit people's food choices with the goal of stopping the epidemic of obesity? For Michael Bloomberg, the former mayor of New York City, the answer is yes. In 2012, he tried to ban large, sugary soft drinks from being sold in the city. However, his proposal was declared unconstitutional by a New York court. Boris Johnson, the prime minister of the United Kingdom, also tried to restrict citizens' food choices. In 2021, he proposed a plan to ban junk food advertisements on TV before 9:00 pm and a total ban online. Critics called the proposal "nutty."

● **For Further Discussion:**

1. Do you think the government should try to limit people's access to unhealthy foods? What policies would you support?
2. Why do people always blame fast food for the problem of rising obesity? How often do you eat fast food?

At present, we humans are facing some huge problems: we have a shortage of water, food, and energy, and at the same time, polluted water, mountains of discarded plastic, and used nuclear fuel rods pose severe dangers for us. Recently, I've won the Nobel Prize for solving these problems, all at the same time. I invented three machines. The first one purifies polluted or radioactive water, so we can drink it at once. The second one changes used plastic into noodles with the help of some chemicals, so we don't have to worry about food shortages. And the last one turns used nuclear fuel rods into firewood, so it can supply adequate and safe energy resources for us.

When I woke up in the morning, I had a horrible headache because I took a couple of sleeping pills last night. And I was so disappointed that I had a vivid, unbelievable DREAM. Anyway, I wonder if my dream will come true.

Topic Preview:

What examples of pollution have you seen in your country? How does pollution affect you personally? What happens to old cell phones, computers, and other electronic items in your country when they are thrown away? Does your country have a ministry of the environment? Do you think they do a good job?

Dialogue:

Joseph: Hey, Donna. Do you have a plastic bag that I can borrow?

Donna: What? I don't have any plastic bags. They have been banned in Canada since 2021.

Joseph: Really? I had no idea. I just need one plastic bag to put some things in.

Donna: Well, I don't have any. Do you still use plastic bags in the US?

Joseph: Yeah, we do. Plastic bags are still used widely in Florida, where I'm from.

Donna: Well, that's a shame. Are there any plans to ban plastic bags in the US?

Joseph: I think there are three states where they are banned, but there is no federal ban at all.

Donna: I find that incredible.

Joseph: Yeah, I guess you're right. We should be doing much more to protect the environment.

Donna: Absolutely! And banning the use of plastic bags is a good place to start.

Pollution

Have you heard about the Great Pacific Garbage Patch? It is a gargantuan collection of plastic trash floating in the North Pacific Ocean. This floating mass of garbage originates from the Pacific Rim, including countries in Asia, North America, and South America. Part of the patch consists of items such as plastic lighters, toothbrushes, water bottles, pens, baby bottles, cell phones, and plastic shopping bags. Many other items are microplastics. The size of the patch is estimated to be double the size of Texas and to contain about 2.7 million metric tons of plastic. Unfortunately, this collection of garbage is rapidly expanding.

Experts estimate that 80% of the plastic in the ocean comes from land-based sources, and 20% comes from boats. Approximately 10,000 shipping containers are lost at sea each year during storms, dropping everything from Lego toys to Nike shoes. A similar patch of floating debris is found in the Atlantic Ocean, and it is dubbed the North Atlantic Garbage Patch. It goes without saying, that this floating garbage is extremely harmful to marine life. It can easily be ingested, causing choking, starvation, and other impairments.

The garbage patch in the Pacific is perhaps the greatest example of human pollution, but is there a way to clean it up? According to Dutch inventor-entrepreneur Boyan Slat, the answer is yes. In 2013, Slat founded an organization called The Ocean Cleanup. Their goal is to remove 90% of floating ocean plastic through the use of a floating barrier that rests on the surface of the water. As it is pushed by wind, waves, and current, it collects ocean debris. After some initial failures, the organization developed a more efficient system that is now in use. It remains to be seen how successful this system will be, but one can be hopeful.

ISSUE 23 POLLUTION

Vocabulary & Expressions:

patch
*a small area that is different from the area around it
- During January, there is usually a *patch* of snow in my front yard.

gargantuan
*very large in size or amount; gigantic
- Tyrannosaurus rex was a *gargantuan* dinosaur that lived more than 65 million years ago.

Pacific Rim
*the countries bordering on or located in the Pacific Ocean
- The *Pacific Rim* stretches from Australia and New Zealand to China to North America and down to South America.

microplastic
*very small fragment of any type of plastic that is less than 5 mm in length
- It is estimated that there are 50 trillion individual pieces of *microplastic* in the world's oceans.

shipping container
*a large reusable metal box used for holding smaller boxes or cartons and designed for easy and fast loading onto a ship, train, or truck
- Standard *shipping containers* are 8 feet (2.4 m) wide, but their length ranges from 10 feet (3 m) to 40 feet (12 m).

debris
*various types of junk or pieces left from something broken down or destroyed
- Floods always leave thousands of pieces of *debris* scattered everywhere.

dub
*to call by a distinctive title or nickname
- Elvis Presley was *dubbed* "the King of Rock and Roll."

it goes without saying
*describing a principle of life that is well known, perfectly clear, or obviously true
- *It goes without saying* that you will receive an automatic zero on a test if the teacher catches you cheating.

ingest
*to take something, such as food, into your body; to swallow something
- Scientists estimate that more than half of the sea turtles worldwide have *ingested* plastic debris.

current
*the fastest part of a stream of sea water
- If you swim in the ocean, you have to be careful that you are not taken out to sea by strong *currents*.

it remains to be seen
*describing something that is not yet clear, certain, or known
- My brother applied for a new job, but *it remains to be seen* if he will get it.

Open to Debate (2): 30 Global Issues

Discussion Points:

1. Are you familiar with the Great Pacific Garbage Patch? Do you think your country contributes to it?
2. Who is responsible for cleaning up ocean garbage? What role should your country play?
3. What is your government doing to keep local rivers and seas free from pollution? Do you think more could be done?
4. Some experts say that the supply of seafood will come to an end around 2048. Do you think this prediction is true? What can we do to prevent it from happening?

Read the following quotes about pollution.
Can you explain what they mean? Do you agree with the idea expressed?

5. If a person poisoned my food, air, or water, they would go to jail. Why can't we stop the companies that poison the world's food, air, and water? Unknown
6. Water and air, the two essential fluids on which all life depends, have become global garbage cans. Jacques Cousteau
7. Pollution should never be the price of prosperity. Al Gore

Current Hot Topic: Plastic Shopping Bags

The modern plastic shopping bag was invented in the 1960s. Beginning in the 1980s, plastic bags became the most common method for carrying purchased items. Plastic bags are 100% recyclable, but many consumers do not recycle them properly. If bags are not recycled, they can take 1,000 years to decompose. Millions of plastic bags make their way into the environment and end up in rivers and oceans, where they are eaten by various sea creatures, leading to their death. While many countries have banned plastic bags entirely, there are some US states where it is legally impossible to ban them.

For Further Discussion:

1. Do stores in your country regularly use plastic bags? Do you think plastic bags should be banned?
2. What are some practical alternatives to plastic bags? Which do you prefer?

India: Do you know what is the most dreadful weapon mankind has ever created? You might think that it's the atomic bomb. You're wrong. It's the "population bomb." You see, most advanced countries are on the decline in population. However, we've already outnumbered China, and our population is still growing. We'll be the only superpower in the world in a couple of decades.

China: Don't get overconfident. We've abolished our one-child policy, and we expect that our population will explode from now on.

Korea: Our population is dwindling away too, and there's no end in sight. We can't rely on an aggressive immigration policy because people actually want to limit immigration. I think unification with North Korea will be the best long-term solution to the current problem.

USA: We aren't worried about population problems because we always accept many legal immigrants, and if we close our eyes for a moment, illegal immigrants will flood into our country. In addition, if the Supreme Court continues to deny abortion rights, our population will multiply rapidly.

Topic Preview:

How would you describe the rate of population growth in your country: fast, moderate, or slow? Are you concerned that the world might become overpopulated during your lifetime? How many brothers and sisters do you have? What is the largest family that you have heard about in your country? What is their life like?

Dialogue:

Richard: Hey, Deborah. Do you know what the current world population is?

Deborah: I think it's around eight billion, but why don't you check worldometers.info? It gives a running total of the global population.

Richard: Okay, thanks. I will check it.

Deborah: By the way, do you know which country has the smallest population?

Richard: Hmmm… that's a tough question. I would guess one of the island countries—maybe Nauru?

Deborah: Haha. Not correct. The world's smallest country is Vatican City.

Richard: Vatican City? You're kidding. That's not a real country!

Deborah: No, it's a real country, recognized by the United Nations. It has about 800 residents.

Richard: Okay, Smarty. Which country will be the world's largest in the year 2030?

Deborah: I think that will be China. They have more people than anyone.

Richard: Not correct! Experts estimate that India will overtake China in population in a few years, so by 2030 the country with the most people will definitely be India.

Deborah: Wow! I had no idea that India's population was expanding that quickly!

ISSUE-24

102 Open to Debate (2): 30 Global Issues

Population Growth

Around 1350, the Black Death came to an end. Since that time, world human population has been growing by leaps and bounds. A mix of advances in agriculture, sanitation, and medicine have reduced mortality and caused this exponential population growth. At present, the global population is increasing by more than 80 million people annually. Experts predict that the population will reach 8.6 billion by 2030, 9.8 billion by 2050, and 11.2 billion by 2100. Meanwhile, some researchers claim that the maximum sustainable population for humans is 8 billion.

In light of these sobering statistics, how many children should a couple have? In some countries, such as South Korea, Japan, Italy, and Portugal, couples are choosing to have one child or none at all. In contrast, there are African countries, such as Nigeria, Mali, Somalia, and Niger, where couples have more than five children. Of course, there are always some men that go far beyond the call of duty and add more to the world's population than one would expect. Consider the case of a man named Ziona, who lived in India and died in 2021. He had 39 wives, 94 children, and 33 grandchildren. He was head of what is thought to be the world's largest family.

What is the solution to a world that seems headed for overpopulation? Researchers say the first step to having smaller families is to empower women and girls. When young women are allowed to pursue education and a career, fertility rates plummet. Second, advanced countries must provide poor countries with more access to contraception to aid in family planning. Third, countries must provide a quality education for all citizens. Women who have a college education have fewer children. Finally, the international community must provide financial aid to help poor countries develop their economies.

ISSUE 24 POPULATION GROWTH

Vocabulary & Expressions:

Black Death — *a severe epidemic of disease that occurred in Asia and Europe in the 14th century
- The **Black Death** caused the death of approximately 200 million people in Eurasia and North Africa from 1346 to 1353.

by leaps and bounds — *with surprisingly fast progress
- Apple Inc. was founded in Steve Jobs's bedroom, but it grew **by leaps and bounds** until it became the world's most valuable company.

mortality — *death rate; the ratio of deaths in a certain area to the population of that area
- The annual *mortality* in the US is about 870 deaths per 100,000 people.

exponential — *characterized by an extremely rapid increase, as in size or extent
- The best example of *exponential* growth is Facebook; it had just one million users in 2004, but now it has about three billion users.

sustainable population — *the maximum population that the world can host
- People who are concerned about the issue of *sustainable population* suggest that couples should not have more than two children.

sobering — *describing something that makes you feel serious and thoughtful
- Here is a *sobering* fact for Americans: drunk driving kills more than 10,000 people every year.

beyond the call of duty — *more than one is required or expected to do
- The police officer received an award for going **beyond the call of duty**.

is thought — *is considered, is believed (by many sources)
- It *is thought* by most scientists that the universe began with the Big Bang about 13.8 billion years ago.

empower — *to give authority or power to someone
- Colleges should *empower* students with the skills necessary to get a job in today's competitive society.

fertility rate — *the average number of children that women of childbearing age give birth to in a specific country.
- At almost seven babies per woman, the country of Niger has the highest *fertility rate* in the world.

plummet — *to decrease suddenly in amount, value, or numbers
- After the CEO was involved in a scandal, the company's stock price *plummeted*.

contraception — *methods that are used to prevent a woman from becoming pregnant; birth control
- The birth control pill is the most common method of *contraception*.

104 Open to Debate (2): 30 Global Issues

Open to Debate (2): 30 Global Issues

Discussion Points:

1. Should the United Nations try to prevent people from having large families, or should they just let people have as many children as they want?
2. What are the advantages and disadvantages of having a lot of children? How many children would you like to have?
3. How many children were in your grandparents' families? What about your parents' families?
4. Nowadays in developed countries, many couples are DINKs ("double income, no kids"). Do you think this is a selfish trend or a personal choice?

Read the following quotes about population growth.
Can you explain what they mean? Do you agree with the idea expressed?

5. Overconsumption and overpopulation underlie every environmental problem we face today. Jacques Cousteau
6. Choosing to have smaller families (one, two, or even no children) is exactly how we end population growth and ultimately achieve a sustainable population on the planet. populationmatters.org
7. The human population can no longer be allowed to grow in the same old uncontrolled way. If we do not take charge of our population size, then nature will do it for us. Sir David Attenborough

Current Hot Topic: Countries with a Low Birth Rate

While the world's population continues to climb, there are some countries where the birth rate is rapidly declining. The best example is South Korea, which needs a total fertility rate of 2.1 to maintain its population. However, in recent years, the rate has dipped below 1.0, the lowest rate within the OECD. If the current rate continues, the Korean people could disappear by 2750. Japan is another example. One expert predicts that if the Japanese birth rate continues to decline, the last Japanese child could be born in the year 3011. Taiwan, Thailand, and Singapore are also at risk.

For Further Discussion:

1. Is it a tragedy if a certain ethnic group disappears, or should we view this event as simply the natural course of life?
2. What actions should countries with a low birth rate take in order to maintain their population levels?

We won't accept same-sex marriage under any circumstances! It's against God's law!

How do you know? Have you really asked your God? If you're not for gay marriage, don't marry a gay person! Period.

Dog: What's all the fuss about? Whether you're in a same-sex or opposite-sex marriage, you both experience the same repercussions of marriage: struggling to get along and often considering divorce. That's why we don't marry; we just have a "brief romance" and go our separate ways.

Why should we need your permission to marry? We don't try to interfere with your marriage, do we?

Topic Preview:

Which countries do you think allow same-sex marriage? Do you think their policy is advanced and enlightened? Which countries do you think prohibit same-sex marriage? Do you know any same-sex couples? What are their lives like?

Dialogue:

Matthew: Hey Jessica. What are your plans for this summer?

Jessica: Well, my biggest plans are to attend my brother's wedding.

Matthew: Oh really? I didn't know he was getting married.

Jessica: Yes, he's been dating a very nice guy from Singapore now for three years.

Matthew: Oh, I didn't know he was gay. Do they plan to get married in Singapore?

Jessica: No, that's impossible. Singapore doesn't recognize same-sex marriage.

Matthew: Oh, sorry to hear that. I thought Singapore was pretty advanced.

Jessica: Well, they are advanced economically, but conservative ideas still control many aspects of the society.

Matthew: I see. Well, where do they plan to get married?

Jessica: Oh, they're getting married in Canada. Same-sex marriage has been legal there since 2005.

Same-Sex Marriage

In 2019, a girl named Sara was born in Spain to a same-sex couple consisting of two women. One mother was born in Bulgaria, and the other was born in Gibraltar, a British territory. Under Spanish law, baby Sara could not get citizenship in Spain because neither of her mothers is of Spanish descent. She could not get British citizenship because people born in Gibraltar cannot transfer citizenship to their children. As a last resort, the Bulgarian mother applied for a birth certificate and citizenship for Sara in Bulgaria. Unfortunately, the Bulgarian constitution defines marriage solely as a union between a man and a woman. In keeping with this provision, Bulgaria summarily refused to issue a birth certificate for Sara, leaving her as a stateless child. Sara was unable to leave Spain because she had no passport to gain admittance to another country.

Most people think of the European Union as one of the main centers of liberal democracy in the world. Bulgaria has been a member of the EU since 2007, but unlike most EU countries, Bulgaria does not recognize same-sex marriage. However, as an EU member, Bulgaria must follow EU rules. Therefore, Sara's mother filed suit against Bulgaria in an EU court. In late 2021, the court ruled that children of same-sex couples recognized in one EU country must be recognized by all EU members. Therefore, Bulgarian authorities had no choice but to issue a passport to Sara, which will be recognized by all EU member states.

Same-sex marriage was first legally permitted in the Netherlands in 2001. Since that time, about thirty countries have legalized the practice. At the other extreme, more than thirty countries have enacted laws that prohibit same-sex marriage. Many other countries allow for civil unions for same-sex couples but not marriage.

ISSUE 25 SAME-SEX MARRIAGE

Vocabulary & Expressions:

descent *referring to a person's ancestors
- The famous actor Robert De Niro is of Italian **descent**.

as a last resort *something you do only if nothing else works; taking your final option after all other options have been used
- Police officers are trained to use their guns only **as a last resort**.

birth certificate *an official document that gives information about a person's birth, including the names of parents, and date, time, and place of birth
- It is usually impossible to get a passport unless you submit your **birth certificate**.

in keeping with *conforming to, agreeing with, or being in compliance with something
- After my grandfather died, his body was cremated, **in keeping with** his wishes.

summarily *in a prompt or direct manner; immediately
- Most professors will **summarily** give a student an F if they learn that he copied his essay from someone else.

stateless *not belonging to a nation; not a citizen of any country
- Albert Einstein gave up his German citizenship to avoid military service; he was **stateless** for five years until he became a Swiss citizen.

liberal democracy *a government in which people elect leaders who believe in the value of social and political change in order to achieve progress
- Australia and New Zealand are good examples of **liberal democracies**.

file suit *to start a legal case against a person or organization; file a lawsuit
- My neighbor damaged my car, but I had to **file suit** to get him to pay for the damage.

have no choice *to be required or forced by law, rules, or circumstances to make a certain decision
- I wanted to study a foreign language, but my school only offered Spanish; I **had no choice** but to take Spanish.

recognize *to accept and approve of something as having legal or official authority
- All countries in the EU must **recognize** same-sex marriages performed in other countries.

enact *to make into law
- Many people believe that the US should **enact** new laws making it more difficult for people to buy guns.

civil union *a legally recognized same-sex relationship that gives the partners some, but not all, of the same rights and responsibilities that married people have
- In Italy, same-sex **civil unions** are permitted but not marriages.

Open to Debate (2): 30 Global Issues

Discussion Points:

1. Does your country permit same-sex marriage? Do you think the law should be changed?
2. Have you ever seen any advertisements in your country featuring same-sex couples? What about TV dramas?
3. Some countries allow for gay people to have a "civil union" but not marriage. Do you think this approach is acceptable?

Read the following quotes about same-sex marriage.
Can you explain what they mean? Do you agree with the idea expressed?

4. I am opposed to same-sex marriage. In the beginning, God created Adam and Eve, not Adam and Steve. Jerry Falwell, conservative pastor
5. I support gay marriage. I believe they have a right to be as miserable as the rest of us. Kinky Friedman
6. Marriage should be about love and respect, not discrimination. That's why I support marriage equality for same-sex couples. Hugh Jackman
7. I believe a marriage isn't between a man and woman, but between love and love. Frank Ocean

● Current Hot Topic: Adoption by Same-Sex Couples

It seems reasonable that if a country permits same-sex marriage, then that country would permit same-sex couples to adopt children. However, that is not always the case. The US legalized same-sex marriage in 2015, so adoptions by same-sex couples are legal nationwide. However, many adoption agencies that are run by religious groups find the idea of gay parenting contrary to their religious beliefs. Therefore, as a matter of conscience, they will not allow same-sex couples to adopt a child. However, research has shown that same-sex couples are just as good at parenting as traditional couples.

● For Further Discussion:

1. Do you think adoption by same-sex couples will ever be allowed in your country? Would you vote to allow it?
2. Some opponents of gay marriage say, "Since children are conceived by a man and a woman, children are therefore entitled to a mother and a father. Thus, single adults and same-sex couples should not be permitted to adopt a child." What is your opinion of this argument?

We have enough money to be able to buy cigarettes and smoke them whenever we want to. Smoking is the best recipe for controlling weight and relieving stress, with no help needed from medicine. I hate to take medicines because they taste bitter and have many side effects.

I can't wait for the day I can smoke as I please. Smokers look cool and intelligent. I'll try to get a job that can allow me to buy cigarettes. But I don't understand one thing: why people in developed countries try to quit smoking. Do they just get tired of smoking, or do drugs give them more pleasure? Anyway, I'll try drugs later after smoking.

Smokers in developing countries are not educated enough to think about the possible repercussions of smoking. They may not be able to enter the stage of a developed country until they realize the bad effects of this terrible habit, so they can actually stop smoking and persuade others to do the same. They should know that becoming a developed country is just as hard as quitting smoking.

Topic Preview:

Why do people smoke? What are the pros and cons of smoking? Do you have any family members or friends who smoke? Have you ever encouraged them to quit? Is it morally wrong for rich countries to export the smoking habit to poor countries?

Dialogue:

Betty: John, I just got a letter from my brother, who's working in Bangladesh.

John: Oh, great! How's he doing?

Betty: He's doing okay. He'll be working there for two years, and then his company will transfer him to another country.

John: I see. Well, he will really get to see many parts of the world.

Betty: Yeah, that's one of the advantages of working for a multinational company.

John: So true. How does he like living in Bangladesh?

Betty: Well, the people are nice, and the cost of living is low, but there is one thing he doesn't like.

John: Yeah? What's that?

Betty: About 60% of the men smoke! It makes life difficult for a nonsmoker.

John: Oh, that's too bad. I've read that nowadays most of the world's smokers are in developing countries.

Betty: Yes, it's true. It's a shame that rich countries are promoting this bad habit to people in poor countries.

John: You can say that again.

Smoking in Developing Countries

Over the past 50 years, the percentage of Americans who smoke has dropped from 42% to 15%. Bans on cigarette advertising, restrictive laws, lawsuits against tobacco companies, and relentless anti-smoking campaigns by health authorities have all served to tighten the noose around smokers. With the decline of smoking in the US, one might think that huge tobacco companies would just go bankrupt. Actually, tobacco companies did two things to make sure their business continued. First, they began to acquire profitable nontobacco businesses. Second, they stepped up their exports of tobacco products to other countries, especially to developing countries. While the level of cigarette consumption has greatly declined in America and Europe, it has risen dramatically in Africa, where it is expected to continue increasing.

Most people know by now that smoking causes numerous deadly diseases, including cancer, heart disease, stroke, diabetes, and various lung diseases. When burned, cigarettes create more than 7,000 chemicals. At least 69 of these chemicals are known to cause cancer, and many are toxic. According to the WHO, the tobacco epidemic is one of the biggest public health threats the world has ever faced. Smoking kills more than eight million people a year around the world. More than seven million of those deaths are the result of direct tobacco use, but more than one million are the result of nonsmokers being exposed to secondhand smoke.

Tobacco growing and consumption have become concentrated in the developing world, where about 80% of smokers live. Studies show that smoking reinforces poverty because low-income smokers spend less on health care, children's education, food, and clothes. Tobacco companies claim that tobacco farming brings positive economic benefits to developing countries, but in fact, most of the profit goes to multinational companies, while many tobacco farmers remain poor and in debt.

ISSUE 26 SMOKING IN DEVELOPING COUNTRIES

Vocabulary & Expressions:

restrictive
*limiting or controlling someone or something
- The state of New York has very *restrictive* rules for cigarette companies; they cannot post an advertisement within 1,500 feet (457 m) of a school.

relentless
*continuing without becoming weaker, slower, or less severe
- Unfortunately, many people were deceived by the *relentless* stream of wrong information about the COVID-19 pandemic.

serve
*to be of use; to fulfill some purpose; to provide some function
- Recent medical research has *served* to confirm my mother's belief that chicken soup is very good for a cold.

tighten the noose
*to make a situation more difficult for someone
- The new tougher penalties will *tighten the noose* on drivers who speed.

go bankrupt
*to be unable to pay one's debts
- In 2020, many cinemas *went bankrupt* because people quit going to the cinema during the COVID-19 pandemic.

acquire
*to come into possession or ownership of something; to get something as one's own
- Philip Morris, the maker of Marlboro cigarettes, *acquired* Kraft Foods in 1988.

step up
*to increase, enlarge, or raise, especially by one or more steps
- Because of high consumer demand, the company s*tepped up* its production of smartphones.

developing country
*a low-income country that is seeking to develop its resources by improving its technology and industry
- *Developing countries* are also called *low-* and *middle-income countries*.

toxic
*containing poisonous or dangerous material
- Nuclear waste must be disposed of carefully; it is highly *toxic* to humans.

concentrated
*existing or happening together in one place; not spread out
- Much of the American development of technology is *concentrated* in Silicon Valley in California.

reinforce
*to strengthen, increase, enlarge, intensify
- UN research *reinforces* the idea that solving global poverty requires the help of many rich nations.

Open to Debate (2): 30 Global Issues

Discussion Points:

1. Why is smoking so popular in developing countries? Shouldn't their governments do more to stop the smoking habit?
2. Some countries, such as Thailand, require cigarette companies to include pictures of throat cancer and mouth cancer on cigarette packs. Do you think this method is an effective warning?
3. What percentage of people are smokers in your country? What has your government done to decrease the smoking habit?
4. What smoking restrictions are in effect in your country nowadays? Do you agree that these restrictions are helpful?

Read the following quotes about smoking.
Can you explain what they mean? Do you agree with the idea expressed?

5. It's easy to quit smoking. I've quit at least a hundred times. Unknown
6. Thousands of people stop smoking every day—by dying from it.
   Anonymous
7. Rather than you smoking a cigarette, the cigarette is really smoking you.
   Anthony Liccione

Current Hot Topic: Avoiding "Sin Stocks"

If you find it shocking that American and European tobacco companies are exporting smoking products to poor countries, what can you do? One step you can take is to avoid investing in "sin stocks." This approach to investing is known as "ethical investing" or "socially responsible investing." Investors who take this approach avoid buying stocks of companies involved in one or more of the following questionable products: alcohol, tobacco, gambling, or pornography. Others will not invest in companies specializing in military equipment, fossil fuel production, or fast food. Strict investors also avoid companies with a record of human rights violations.

For Further Discussion:

1. Among the products listed in the reading, which ones would you never invest in? Which ones do you think are acceptable as investments?
2. Is it ever morally acceptable to invest in "sin stocks"? What if you can earn a lot of money and donate part of it to charity?

— Finally, my dream has come true. I have a grand house, a chauffeured limousine, and lots of money to spend for the rest of my life.
— Really? I envy you. Then why are you still living with your parents? Why don't you move out?
— No way!
— Why not?
— The computer I'm using is my dad's.
— Do you mean you're living in virtual reality?
— Yes. But I don't care because I've succeeded in my life ANYWAY.
— I'm sorry to hear that you're living in such a dreamworld.

LIFE IS BETTER IN VIRTUAL WORLD!

Son, get out of the monitor immediately. We're supposed to meet your doctor at two, and we're late. Hurry up!

Topic Preview:

Do you have a social media account? How much time do you spend on it? Do you think that social media has had a positive effect on society? Do you follow any celebrities on social media?

Dialogue:

Barbara: Michael, do you have a social media account?

Michael: Yeah, I have a Facebook account, but I haven't posted anything.

Barbara: Really? Why not?

Michael: It's just not my thing. The only reason that I created an account was just to see pictures of my nephew and niece that my sister posts.

Barbara: I see. Well, could I have your Facebook address? I want to add you to our class list.

Michael: Okay. I'll write it down for you. By the way, how many social media accounts do you have?

Barbara: Well, I'm pretty active on social media. I'm on Facebook, Twitter, Instagram, YouTube, and WhatsApp.

Michael: Wow! That's a lot! You must stay pretty busy. How do you find time for your private life?

Barbara: I limit my social media activities to about ten hours per week, so that leaves plenty of time to meet my friends and family.

Michael: I see. Well, just don't become obsessed with social media.

Barbara: Don't worry! I've got everything under control.

Social Media

In the small city of Sidi Bouzid, Tunisia, police officers targeted and mistreated a street vendor named Mohamed Bouazizi for years, routinely confiscating his small cart of produce. On December 17, 2010, he started his day normally, but just after 10:30 am, the police began harassing him, ostensibly because he did not have a vendor's permit. In reality, no permit was needed if a person sold produce from a cart. The police officials demanded a bribe, but Bouazizi had no money. He was publicly humiliated, his electronic weighing scales were confiscated, and his produce cart was tossed aside. Left with no way to make a living, a distraught Bouazizi bought some gasoline, poured it on himself, and set himself on fire. He later died in a hospital.

Public anger toward the authorities intensified after Bouazizi's death. People in Tunisia began to lash out against their corrupt and oppressive government. They started a movement known as the Arab Spring, which quickly spread to Egypt, Libya, Syria, and other countries. The movement was led by young people who used social media, including Facebook, Twitter, and YouTube, to organize themselves and work toward a common goal. They spread their message to people all over the world, garnering global support that led to the downfall of the Tunisian government and others.

The Arab Spring is a practical illustration of the positive power of social media to bring down authoritarian governments. When used in reasonable ways, social media can bring about beneficial changes in society. Unfortunately, social media also has a dark side. It can endanger the lives of journalists and activists, be used to commit crimes, and foster cyberbullying. In addition, for many young people, social media creates feelings of inferiority, causes episodes of depression, and leads to lower academic performance.

ISSUE 27 SOCIAL MEDIA

Vocabulary & Expressions:

target
*to aim an attack at someone or something
- Robbers on the street usually *target* people who are walking alone.

confiscate
*to take something away from someone, especially to enforce the law or rules
- The police *confiscated* the car when they discovered it was stolen.

harass
*to annoy or bother someone in a constant or repeated way
- The secretary complained that another employee was *harassing* her, continually asking her for a date.

ostensibly
*apparently, seemingly
- The politician was *ostensibly* generous, giving much to charity; however, his real purpose was to become more popular with voters.

distraught
*very upset; so upset that you are not able to think clearly or behave normally
- My father was *distraught* when he lost his job.

intensified
*made stronger or more extreme
- When John's wife found out that he lied about being at a business meeting, her anger *intensified*.

lash out
*to make a sudden and angry attack against
- Citizens usually *lash out* against the government when taxes are increased.

oppressive
*severe, cruel, harsh, or unkind without good reason
- The workers complained about the new boss's *oppressive* rules.

garner
*to acquire or earn
- BTS has *garnered* worldwide support because of their singing and dancing skills as well as their charm.

bring down
*to cause something to fall, collapse, or die
- The president was well liked at first, but a scandal later *brought down* his government.

dark side
*the parts of a person, a group, an activity, company, or other thing that are unpleasant, evil, or harmful
- The police chief does a good job, but he has a *dark side* in that he sometimes takes bribes.

activist
*a person who uses strong actions, such as public protests, to help make changes in politics or society
- Labor *activists* protested in front of the company offices until working conditions were improved.

foster
*to help the growth and development of something
- Good parents *foster* a sense of respect for others in their children.

Open to Debate (2): 30 Global Issues

Open to Debate (2): 30 Global Issues

Discussion Points:

1. How has social media been used in a positive way to bring about social change in your country?
2. What are the greatest benefits of social media? What are its worst aspects?
3. Some people say that social media is addictive like a drug. Do you agree with this idea?
4. Do you know anyone who spends too much time on social media? What is their life like?

Read the following quotes about social media.
Can you explain what they mean? Do you agree with the idea expressed?

5. The great thing about social media is how it gives a voice to voiceless people. Jon Ronson
6. When you are happy with someone in private, you don't need to prove it on social media. Unknown
7. Some people need to realize that Facebook is a social network, not a diary. Unknown

Current Hot Topic: Fake News on Social Media

While social media provides many benefits to society, it also provides an opportunity for dishonest people to spread fake news. It is a fact that the coronavirus arrived in 2020. This deadly disease quickly spread around the world, killing millions. Many people turned to social media for their medical news. Sadly, they found an incredible amount of fake news, ranging from the assertion that the coronavirus was fake to the unbelievable claim that the COVID-19 vaccines contain microchips. Facebook reported that in the first year of the COVID pandemic, it removed 18 million posts containing fake news about the virus.

For Further Discussion:

1. Have you ever seen any fake news on social media? What were the claims? How did you know it was fake news?
2. What are your main sources of daily news? Who do you rely on for medical information?

Years ago, I decided to give up my life, and I ordered a pizza for my last meal. It was so delicious that I wanted to know the recipe. I visited the pizzeria and asked about the pizza.
— I want to know your pizza recipe. Could you give it to me?
— It's our business secret. But if you work here for a year, we'll give you the recipe.

I worked there for a year and started my own food truck business. It was a huge success because so many suicidal people are out there, looking for some enjoyment in life.

I never dreamed that there's a pizza for suicidal people. I hope this pizza will give me hope, so I can return to my happy life.

I suspect this is one of the owner's business tactics. But I have no choice but to buy his pizza because I'm tempted to take my life every day.

Topic Preview:

How would you describe the suicide rate in your country: high, moderate, low? Have you ever read about a celebrity who committed suicide? Why would they do such a terrible thing? When you feel discouraged, what are the moral or spiritual principles that keep you moving forward in life?

Dialogue:

Ashley: Hey, Robert. Can you join our class party on Friday night?

Robert: Oh, sorry. I have plans already.

Ashley: I see. What's up? Do you have a date?

Robert: Not at all. I work as a volunteer for a suicide hotline.

Ashley: Oh, wow! That's really impressive. How often do you do that?

Robert: Well, like you, I'm a busy student. I just have time to work on the hotline two nights per week.

Ashley: That's very admirable of you to help others.

Robert: Thanks, but I have a very special motivation.

Ashley: Really? What's that?

Robert: My brother attempted suicide a few years ago, so I became very concerned about this matter and want to help others.

Ashley: I see. Well, is he okay now?

Robert: Yes, thank God that he managed to get some help for his depression, and he's doing okay now.

Ashley: Good to hear! Well, I wish you well on your volunteer work. You can join a class party another time.

Robert: Thanks.

Suicide

The whole world was shocked and dismayed when the deadly coronavirus struck the planet in early 2020. Not only did the virus kill millions of people, it inflicted immense psychological harm. In January 2021, a mother in Tokyo tested positive for the coronavirus, though she showed no symptoms. She self-isolated at her home because many hospitals were overloaded with COVID-19 patients, and thousands of residents were on waiting lists to be admitted. The frantic mother became worried that she might have transmitted the virus to her daughter. In her distress, she saw no way out, and she made the ghastly decision to take her own life. She was not alone. Approximately 325 Japanese people commit suicide every day.

Japan is not the only country that has a high rate of suicide. Since the early 2000s, South Korea, has had the highest rate of suicide among OECD members, except for a couple of years when Lithuania eclipsed them for this dubious honor. The tendency to view suicide as a solution to life's problems affects all of Korean society. Students who do not perform well on the college entrance exam may feel as though they have shamed the family, leading them to take their own life. Even celebrities are not exempt from this scourge. In 2017, Kim Jonghyun, a member of the South Korean group Shinee, died by suicide at the age of 27. In a suicide note, he used such expressions as "I am broken inside" and "I hate myself."

According to the WHO, more than 700,000 people commit suicide every year. For every suicide, there are many more people who attempt suicide. In fact, the most important risk factor for suicide is a prior suicide attempt. Suicide is the fourth leading cause of death among 15–19 year olds.

ISSUE 28 SUICIDE

Vocabulary & Expressions:

dismayed *being upset, worried, or agitated because of some unwelcome situation or occurrence
- My parents were *dismayed* when my little brother was caught smoking at school.

inflict *to cause someone to experience something unpleasant or harmful
- Yelling at employees *inflicts* excessive mental stress on them.

overload *to put an excessive burden on someone or something
- The ship sank because it was *overloaded* with heavy items.

frantic *feeling or showing fear and worry
- After my mother lost a $100 bill, she engaged in a *frantic* search until she found it.

transmit *to cause a virus or disease to be given to others
- Experts believe that an animal may have first *transmitted* the coronavirus to humans at a market that sold live animals.

way out *a solution to a serious problem
- Nowadays, many people have so much debt that they can see no *way out* of their financial problems.

ghastly *very shocking or horrible
- Slavery was a *ghastly* practice in America that existed from 1619 to 1865.

eclipse *to do better than; to defeat or outdo
- In the 2020 Summer Olympics, Korean archer An San *eclipsed* all opponents to win the gold medal in the women's individual archery event.

dubious honor *a doubtful or questionable award
- Linda Wolfe holds the *dubious honor* for being the most married woman in the world; she was married a total of 23 times.

shame *to cause others to feel guilt, regret, embarrassment, or dishonor
- In some cultures, if young people don't get married by age 30, they have *shamed* their parents.

exempt from *free from some requirement that other persons must meet
- Most American universities require applicants to take the SAT; no one is *exempt from* taking it.

risk factor *something that increases risk, especially something that makes a person more likely to get a particular disease or get involved in a particular negative activity
- Losing one's job is a significant *risk factor* for suicide.

Open to Debate (2): 30 Global Issues

Discussion Points:

1. Why do people make the terrible decision to take their own lives?
2. Do you know anyone who committed suicide or attempted to commit suicide? What sort of problems did they have?
3. If your best friend talked about committing suicide, what advice would you give?
4. Does your country have a suicide hotline? Do you think it's effective in preventing suicides?

Read the following quotes about suicide.
Can you explain what they mean? Do you agree with the idea expressed?

5. The only difference between suicide and martyrdom is press coverage.
   Chuck Palahniuk
6. But in the end, one needs more courage to live than to kill himself.
   Albert Camus
7. When people kill themselves, they think they're ending the pain, but all they're doing is passing it on to those they leave behind. Jeannette Walls

Current Hot Topic: Religious Views on Suicide

Buddhism observes that the reasons for suicide are negative, and thus it counteracts the path to enlightenment. In Hinduism, taking your own life is considered a violation of the code of nonviolence. According to both Catholic and Protestant churches, suicide violates the commandment "You shall not murder" (Exodus 20:13). Islam clearly forbids suicide: "And do not kill yourselves; surely God is most merciful to you" (Koran 4:29). The views of Judaism on suicide are mixed. In Orthodox Judaism, suicide is strictly forbidden as a sin. Other forms of Judaism tend to view suicide as a death caused by a disease.

For Further Discussion:

1. Do you think that committing suicide is a sin? Is it an unforgivable sin?
2. In your view, what happens when we die? Do you think that heaven and hell are real places?

— We're arresting you.
— What for? I did nothing wrong!
— You know we have CCTVs everywhere, and we saw you buy a knife at the market.
— That's right. I'm on my way to my girlfriend's house, and we're going to make some sandwiches for lunch. It's just a bread knife.
— You're lying! We know you have a plan to murder your girlfriend after lunch.
— What? I have no idea what you're talking about!
— Don't try to fool us! We have undeniable evidence.
— What evidence? Tell me!
— Recently, we've introduced some state-of-the-art CCTVs, and they can READ YOUR MIND as well as show your movements. That's why we're arresting you for ATTEMPTED MURDER.

Topic Preview:

Do you think that the increasing number of CCTV cameras is a good trend in our society, or do you think we already have enough? What sort of places should have CCTV cameras (e.g., banks)? What kinds of places should never have a CCTV camera (e.g., saunas)? Do police in your city use cameras to catch speeders? Do you think that's an appropriate use of technology?

Dialogue:

Amanda: William, you won't believe what happened to me!

William: I have no idea. Tell me!

Amanda: Somehow a thief got my credit card number and started using it.

William: Oh my! Did he steal your actual card?

Amanda: No, he didn't. He must have gotten the number and made a new card with it. Now he's trying to charge things all over town.

William: Well, you cancelled the card, didn't you?

Amanda: Yes, I cancelled it this morning as soon as my bank called me about some suspicious purchases.

William: Well, that's good. At least he can't charge anything else.

Amanda: Right! Also, I've made a report to the police. I hope they catch the guy soon.

William: Well, nowadays, almost every store has CCTV. If the police just check the store's cameras, they should be able to get an image of him and catch him.

Amanda: I hope you're right!

Surveillance and Privacy

One day in the autumn of 2021, a homeowner who lived in Peterborough, England, woke up to find his garden gate was open. He always kept the gate closed, so he immediately knew that something was amiss. He checked his CCTV cameras and spotted the culprit. He saw that a man had entered the garden and was trying unsuccessfully to open doors of the house. The homeowner notified the police, who then checked the video footage. It turned out that the would-be burglar was a 21-year-old career criminal. The man was immediately arrested and charged with "attempted burglary." Having been caught red-handed on CCTV, the man admitted to his crime and was sentenced to a year in prison.

The number of CCTVs in use is increasing daily. In the UK, there are more than five million CCTV cameras in use, which is the equivalent of one camera for every 13 people. However, about 96% of these surveillance cameras are owned by private businesses and homeowners, who use them as a deterrent to criminal activity. According to British police, the escalating use of CCTVs represents a major breakthrough in reducing crime.

While surveillance cameras help in reducing crime, privacy advocates claim that the constant use of CCTVs can get out of hand and violate people's right to privacy. Critics cite China as an example. China has more CCTVs than any country in the world. Major cities in China have more than one camera for every citizen, so every citizen is constantly under surveillance. In addition, every citizen's online life is constantly monitored. Facebook, Twitter, and Google are banned. Instead, citizens must use local social media sites, like Sina Weibo and RenRen. The government can delete posts as they see fit. Those who post false statements can be sent to prison.

ISSUE 29 SURVEILLANCE AND PRIVACY

Vocabulary & Expressions:

amiss — *when something is not right, proper, or in correct order
- As soon as I entered my room, I knew that something was *amiss*; my laptop was not in its normal place.

culprit — *a person who has committed a crime or done something wrong
- My bicycle was stolen last week, but the police found the *culprit* and arrested him.

would-be — *wishing or pretending to be
- My brother is a *would-be* comedian; he's always telling jokes and trying to make people laugh.

burglar — *a person who breaks into a building, especially at night, with the intent to steal things
- The *burglar* stole a computer, but he was identified on the homeowner's CCTV and arrested.

career criminal — *a person who has committed many crimes throughout his or her life
- Carl Gugasian is one of the most well-known *career criminals*; he robbed more than 50 banks during his lifetime.

red-handed — *observed in the act of doing something wrong
- The student was caught *red-handed* when he copied an answer from his friend's test.

deterrent — *something that makes someone decide not to commit a crime or do something bad
- Car alarms are an important *deterrent* against theft.

escalate — *to become greater, higher, worse, or more severe
- With the current shortage of police officers, crime has been *escalating* in our city.

breakthrough — *a sudden advance or successful development
- Local scientists have announced a *breakthrough* in medical research on viruses.

get out of hand — *to become out of control; to go beyond reasonable limits
- When my neighbors were out of town, their teenage son had a huge party, which quickly *got out of hand*.

monitor — *to check, watch, or keep track of, usually for a special purpose
- When my grandfather was in the hospital, the nurses *monitored* his heart rate continuously.

as one sees fit — *to choose to do something because one thinks it is right, appropriate, or desirable
- Children can spend their birthday money *as they see fit*.

Open to Debate (2): 30 Global Issues

Discussion Points:

1. What are the advantages of having many surveillance cameras around? What are the disadvantages?
2. Does your city have a lot of surveillance cameras? What types of places usually have them?
3. Have you heard about any cases where a criminal was caught on camera? What happened?
4. Are there any surveillance cameras near your home? How do you feel when you see them?

Read the following quotes about surveillance and privacy.
Can you explain what they mean? Do you agree with the idea expressed?

5. We are rapidly entering the age of no privacy, where everyone is open to surveillance at all times, where there are no secrets from government.
   William O. Douglas
6. Surveillance is the business model of the Internet. Bruce Schneier
7. Facebook is not your friend; it is a surveillance engine. Richard Stallman

Current Hot Topic: Cell Phone Surveillance

Many law enforcement agencies in Canada, the US, and the UK are now using an electronic device called a StingRay. It acts like a cell phone tower and catches local cell phone signals. Police officials say that it is a great crime-fighting device, but privacy advocates point out that the device is often used without a warrant from a court, which violates privacy laws. Numerous court cases have been brought in the US in an attempt to stop the use of StingRays as a violation of a person's right to privacy. However, they are still widely used.

For Further Discussion:

1. Do you know if police in your area use the StingRay or a similar device? Do you think the use of such devices is a violation of a person's right to privacy?
2. Have you ever wondered if someone was intercepting your cell phone calls or messages? What happened?

— Freeze! One more move, and I'll shoot!
— Go ahead! Don't you see I'm wearing a suicide vest? If you do, we'll all die together!
— Take off your jacket right now! This is a clear-cut act of TERRORISM!
— Terrorism? I don't think so. I'm waging a WAR against you. We can't afford tanks, missiles, and guns. That's why we're fighting with this suicide vest. It's our last weapon left.
— It's a WAR CRIME!
— War crime? What kills more people, your tanks and missiles or my suicide vest?
— Listen! We call the "biggest killing" a WAR while the "smallest one" is a CRIME.

Topic Preview:

How do you feel when you read about acts of terrorism in other countries? Does it make you feel reluctant to travel to those countries? Why do people choose terrorism instead of democratic methods? What are the most effective ways to stop terrorism?

Dialogue:

Mary: Hey, James. I need your help. I'm writing an essay about terrorism.

James: Yeah? What do you need help with?

Mary: Well, you're from Canada, which is well known as a peaceful country. How does your government protect the people from terrorism?

James: Yes, of course, Canada is recognized as a nonviolent society, but we still experience acts of domestic terrorism.

Mary: Really? Can you cite some examples?

James: Well, in 2017, a racist gunman from Quebec City entered a Muslim mosque and killed six people.

Mary: Oh, my! That's terrible!

James: Then in 2021, another Canadian man drove a pickup truck into a Muslim family that was just walking down the street. He killed four people from the same family.

Mary: I guess no country is safe from terrorism—not even a peace-loving country like Canada.

James: Truer words were never spoken.

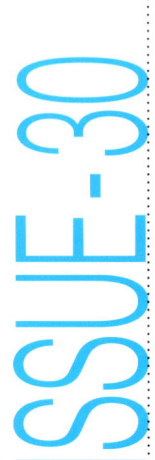

Terrorism

November 13, 2015, began as a normal day in Paris, the most famous center of culture and cuisine in the world. All of the pleasant tranquility in the city came to an end at 9:15 pm, when three suicide bombers struck outside a stadium during an international football match. A second group of attackers then fired on crowded cafés and restaurants. A third group conducted another mass shooting and took hostages at a rock concert attended by 1,500 people. At the end of the day, the appalling death toll reached 130 people, including 90 at the theater. Another 416 people were injured. Seven of the terrorists were also killed. The attacks were the deadliest in France since World War II. It was now crystal clear that no city in the world was safe from terrorism, not even the City of Light.

What motivated the attackers to carry out such senseless carnage? The Islamic State (ISIL) claimed responsibility for the attacks, saying that they were carried out in revenge for French airstrikes on ISIL sites in Syria and Iraq. It turned out that the attacks were planned in Syria and organized by a terrorist cell based in Belgium. Two of the attackers were Iraqis, but most were born in France or Belgium and had fought in the war in Syria. In response to the attacks, France declared a three-month state of emergency. On November 18, the suspected leader of the attacks was killed in a police raid, along with two others. At the same time, France launched some of its biggest airstrikes against ISIL sites.

The shocking attacks in Paris are just one example of the continuing global battle against terrorism. The Global Terrorism Database now contains information on more than 200,000 terrorist attacks that have been carried out since 1970.

ISSUE 30 TERRORISM

Vocabulary & Expressions:

cuisine — *a manner or style of preparing food
- Korean *cuisine* is often very spicy.

tranquility — *the quality or state of being calm, peaceful, and quiet
- My grandfather had a stressful job; he did not find a life of *tranquility* until he retired.

suicide bomber — *a person who commits suicide by exploding a bomb in order to kill other people
- On July 7, 2005, four *suicide bombers* carried out attacks on public transportation in London, killing 52 residents and themselves.

hostage — *a person who is captured by someone who demands that money be paid or certain actions be taken before the captured person is freed
- The terrorists demanded a plane, a pilot, and money in exchange for the *hostages*.

appalling — *being shocking and terrible
- The homeless man was found living in *appalling* conditions.

death toll — *the number of people who die in an accident, disaster, war, or terrorist act
- When the Titanic sank on April 15, 1912, the *death toll* topped 1,500.

crystal clear — *perfectly easy to understand
- My teacher was *crystal clear* about the homework; there was no way any student could misunderstand.

terrorism — *the use of violent acts to frighten the people in an area as a way of trying to achieve a political or religious goal
- The Global Terrorism Database includes information about various acts of *terrorism*, including more than 80,000 bombings.

City of Light — *a nickname for Paris, France
- Paris is called the *City of Light* because of its leading role during the Age of Enlightenment (about 1685-1815).

carnage — *the killing of many people
- On September 11, 2001, terrorists attacked the United States, killing almost 3,000 people; Al-Qaeda claimed responsibility for the *carnage*.

Islamic State (ISIL) — *the Islamic State of Iraq and the Levant (ISIL); AKA the Islamic State of Iraq and Syria (ISIS) or *Daesh*; a militant Islamic group that controlled part of Iraq and Syria from 2014 to 2019
- The *Islamic State* has been designated as a terrorist organization by the United Nations.

state of emergency — *a situation of extreme danger or threat of danger to a nation from foreign or domestic sources
- During a *state of emergency*, the police have special powers to enter people's homes and to arrest people.

Open to Debate (2): *30 Global Issues*

Discussion Points:

1. What motivates terrorists to commit terrible acts of violence? Why would anyone volunteer to be a suicide bomber?
2. What are the most effective ways of stopping terrorism before it happens?
3. Have any citizens of your country been victims of terrorist attacks in other countries? What happened?

Read the following quotes about terrorism.
Can you explain what they mean? Do you agree with the idea expressed?

4. With guns you can kill terrorists; with education you can kill terrorism.
   Malala Yousafzai
5. You cannot win a War on Terrorism. It's like having a war on jealousy.
   David Cross
6. If we destroy human rights and rule of law in the response to terrorism, they have won. Joichi Ito
7. No religion is responsible for terrorism. People are responsible for violence and terrorism. Barack Obama

Current Hot Topic: Domestic Terrorism

Acts of terrorism can easily be carried out by a country's own citizens. Such violence is called "homegrown terrorism" or "domestic terrorism." In 2011, an anti-Muslim terrorist in Norway killed 77 people. In 2014, eight knife-wielding terrorists killed 31 civilians at the Kunming railway station in China. In 2017, an Islamist extremist suicide bomber detonated a bomb in Manchester, England, which killed 23 people. In 2019, an anti-Muslim New Zealander killed 51 people at an Islamic Center. In 2020, the FBI arrested 13 American men who had plotted to kidnap Gretchen Whitmer, the governor of Michigan.

For Further Discussion:

1. Can you think of any recent examples of domestic terrorism in your country? What happened?
2. What department of your country's government protects the people from terrorism, either foreign or domestic? Do you think they do a good job?

Notes about Grammar and Style

The purpose of this appendix is to make a few observations about grammar and style that users of this book may find helpful.

1. American English

There are many varieties of English in use in the world, but the two that are found most often are American English and British English. It is best to view these as two models for learning English. In many parts of the world, British English is the preferred model; in other areas, American English is preferred. It is best to choose one model and stick with it. In this book, we follow the American English model.

2. Abbreviations

We use few abbreviations in this book, but it will be helpful to list them here.

AKA	also known as
e.g.	*exempli gratia*, a Latin expression that means "for example." This expression is used when you want to cite an example of something.
etc.	*et cetera*, a Latin expression that means "and the rest." In modern usage, etc. means "and so on" or "and so forth." This expression is used at the end of a list to show that other things could be added to the list.
i.e.	*id est*, a Latin expression meaning "that is" or "in other words."

3. Styles of Writing

When writing in English, how do you know when to use a comma, hyphen, and other marks of punctuation? To answer specific questions about punctuation, spelling, use of numbers, and other matters of style, it is best to choose a style guide to follow. If you are taking an English writing class, your teacher may ask you to follow a specific guide. Four main styles exist in modern English writing.

AP	*Associated Press Stylebook*	Newspaper style
APA	*Publication Manual of the American Psychological Association*	Science style
CMOS	*The Chicago Manual of Style*	Book-editing style
MLA	*MLA Handbook* [Modern Language Association of America]	Academic style

In this book, we mostly follow the *CMOS* style.

One of the unique aspects of *CMOS* style lies in the way it uses hyphens. In many cases, a hyphen is used in a compound adjective when it appears before a noun, but not when it occurs after a noun. Thus, the hyphen is omitted in the second example below, even though dictionaries show the word *well-known* with a hyphen.

> John is a *well-known* teacher.
> John is *well known* in the community.

If you would like to learn the *CMOS* rules about using hyphens, just google "*CMOS* hyphen style guide," and you will be able to find a chart showing all the *CMOS* rules.

4. Spelling

Many English words have alternate spellings. For example, which of the following words is spelled correctly: *lifestyle*, *life style*, *life-style*? If you consult Dictionary.com, you will see all three spellings listed as possibilities, though *lifestyle* is the first one listed. If you consult Merriam-Webster.com, you find only the spelling *lifestyle*. Likewise, which is the correct spelling: *smartphone* or *smart phone*? Both are possible, but *smartphone* is the preferred spelling according to Merriam-Webster. For matters of spelling in this book, we follow Merriam-Webster.com

5. Gender Neutrality

Before the 1970s, writers often used the pronouns *he/him/his* in a generic sense to represent both genders. It was common to read sentences like this:

> If a student wants to get an A+, *he* must turn in all *his* homework on time.

In this sentence, *he* represents *he or she*, and *his* represents *his or her*. However, many writers object to this generic use of *he* to represent both genders as a sexist practice. Therefore, since the 1970s, writers have used various techniques to avoid such gender-biased language.

APPENDIX

In this book, we use a variety of methods to express gender. In some cases, we use *he/his/him* in a generic sense to refer to either gender:

Would you vote for a politician in *his* 70s or 80s?

In other cases, we use *she/her* in a generic sense to refer to either gender:

If a teacher is kind, *her* students will experience bonding with *her*.

Sometimes, we use *he or she*:

Do you think *he or she* [a highly paid CEO] is worth that much money?

We also use modern gender-neutral words for occupations instead of old-fashioned, gender-biased words. The words in the first column below are preferred.

fisher	fisherman
firefighter	fireman
police officer	policeman
server	waiter/waitress
host	host/hostess

We use *they/them/their* where the gender of a person could be male or female.

When a driver is using the autopilot feature, *they* must still pay attention to driving.

Do you know anyone who is a vegetarian? What are *their* reasons for choosing that lifestyle?

Some writers object to the use of *they* to represent *he/she* and *their* to represent *his/her*. However, Michael Swan points out:

This use of *they/them/their* has existed for centuries and is perfectly correct. It is most common in an informal style, but can also be found in formal written English (*Practical English Usage*, 3rd ed. Oxford University Press, 2005, p. 521).

6. Capitalization of Black

In 2020, the Associated Press announced that it was making a major change in the *AP Stylebook*. Going forward, the news organization would capitalize the "b" in the word *Black* when the word was used to refer to people in a racial, ethnic, or cultural context.

APPENDIX

A spokesperson for the AP said that the change was intended to convey a shared sense of history and identity that exists among Black people. He added, "The lowercase *black* is a color, not a person."

In addition to capitalizing the word Black when referring to *Black* people, the *AP* said that it would also capitalize the word *Indigenous* when it was used to refer to the original inhabitants of a place. However, the *AP* stated that it would not capitalize the word *brown*, which has sometimes been used to refer to Latinos. The *AP* added that writers should avoid using the word *brown* to refer to people, describing the word as a broad and imprecise term for the purpose of making racial, ethnic, or cultural references.

The *AP Stylebook*'s new policy also stated that the word *white* should not be capitalized when referring to white people. The *AP* pointed out that white people have less of a shared history and culture than Black people, and white people don't generally have the experience of being discriminated against because of skin color.

Following the changes in the *AP Stylebook*, numerous news organizations have also changed their style guides to capitalize *Black*, including the *Los Angeles Times*, *Boston Globe*, *Seattle Times*, and *USA Today*. The *CMOS* also announced that they now recommend capitalizing *Black* when it refers to people in a racial or ethnic sense.

Other news organizations, such as CNN and Fox News, announced that they would also capitalize the word *white* when it referred to white people as a racial group. They explained that capitalizing *white* was consistent with the capitalization of Black, Asian, Latino, and other ethnic groups.

In this book, we capitalize *Black* and *Indigenous* when referring to people as a racial group. However, we do not capitalize *white* and *brown*.

What's Inside

Open to Debate 1 30 Korean Issues

Issue 01	BTS
Issue 02	Corruption and Transparency
Issue 03	COVID-19
Issue 04	Digital Sex Crimes
Issue 05	Divorce
Issue 06	Dog Meat
Issue 07	Drinking Culture
Issue 08	Health Supplements
Issue 09	High Cost of Dying
Issue 10	Housing Bubble
Issue 11	International Workers
Issue 12	LGBTQ
Issue 13	Low Birth Rate
Issue 14	North Korea, China, and Japan
Issue 15	Obsession with Sports
Issue 16	Planning for Retirement
Issue 17	Plastic Surgery
Issue 18	Rising Crime Rate
Issue 19	Rising Obesity
Issue 20	Scams and More Scams
Issue 21	Sexual Harassment
Issue 22	Smartphone Addiction
Issue 23	Suicide
Issue 24	Tattoo Artistry
Issue 25	The Republic of Seoul
Issue 26	Too Much Work
Issue 27	Traffic Accidents
Issue 28	TV Dramas
Issue 29	Value of a College Education
Issue 30	Where to Invest

Open to Debate 3 30 Money Issues

Issue 01	A Country Goes Bankrupt?
Issue 02	A Delivery War among Supermarkets
Issue 03	Aging Populations
Issue 04	American Greed
Issue 05	Bitcoin
Issue 06	Credit Card Debt
Issue 07	Cybersecurity and Your Money
Issue 08	Dog Day Care
Issue 09	Drinking and Productivity
Issue 10	Educated but Unemployed
Issue 11	Excessive Compensation for CEOs
Issue 12	Future Energy
Issue 13	Global Trade Protectionism
Issue 14	Governmental Control of Obesity
Issue 15	Home Ownership
Issue 16	Internet Millionaire
Issue 17	Jobs of the Future
Issue 18	Labor Unions
Issue 19	Leaving Money to Your Children
Issue 20	Loaning Money to Family and Friends
Issue 21	Money and Happiness
Issue 22	National Pension Plans
Issue 23	Sexual Harassment in the Workplace
Issue 24	Student Loans and Student Debt
Issue 25	The Business of Corruption
Issue 26	The Frenzy of Black Friday
Issue 27	The Lottery
Issue 28	The Power of Inflation
Issue 29	The World's Most Expensive Health Care
Issue 30	Wealth Inequality

Open to Debate 4 30 Cultural Issues

Issue 01	Alcohol
Issue 02	Babysitting
Issue 03	Breastfeeding
Issue 04	Bribery
Issue 05	Cell Phones
Issue 06	Clothing
Issue 07	Cost of Health Care
Issue 08	Crime and Punishment
Issue 09	Dating
Issue 10	Driving
Issue 11	Funerals and Burial
Issue 12	Gender Roles
Issue 13	Gestures and Body Language
Issue 14	LGBTQ Rights
Issue 15	Marriage and Divorce
Issue 16	Obesity
Issue 17	Personal Space
Issue 18	Public Display of Affection
Issue 19	Public Nudity
Issue 20	Racism
Issue 21	Retirement
Issue 22	Shopping
Issue 23	Smoking Bans
Issue 24	Strange Laws
Issue 25	Superstitions
Issue 26	Time and Punctuality
Issue 27	Tipping
Issue 28	Toilets
Issue 29	Weddings
Issue 30	Work and Vacations

Open to Debate 5 30 American Issues

Issue 01	Abortion
Issue 02	Age Discrimination
Issue 03	Anti-Vaxxers
Issue 04	Black Lives Matter
Issue 05	Breastfeeding in Public
Issue 06	CEO Salaries
Issue 07	College Admissions
Issue 08	Death Penalty
Issue 09	Drug Dependence
Issue 10	DUI
Issue 11	Equal Justice
Issue 12	FBI Surveillance
Issue 13	Fraud
Issue 14	Gender Diversity
Issue 15	Gun Violence
Issue 16	Health Care
Issue 17	Hot Car Death
Issue 18	Immigration
Issue 19	Police Brutality
Issue 20	Poverty
Issue 21	Racially Motivated Violence
Issue 22	Rich Pastors
Issue 23	Risky Activities
Issue 24	Road Rage
Issue 25	Same-Sex Marriage
Issue 26	Service Dogs
Issue 27	Student Loans
Issue 28	Transgender People
Issue 29	Universal Basic Income
Issue 30	White Supremacy

DISCUSSION TEXTBOOK
FROM LIS KOREA

중고급 어린이들을 위한 독창적인 영어교재

New Children's Talk (1), (2), (3)

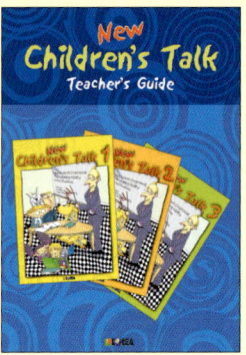

교사용

New Children's Talk (TG)

- 일상생활에서 벌어지는 상황들을 다양한 포맷에 맞추어서 많은 Speaking Chance를 제공합니다.
- 암기 위주의 영어가 아니라 자기 의견을 만들어 낼 수 있는 포맷들을 제공합니다.

청소년의 세계와 그들의 생각 관심사들을 토론으로

Chat Room for Teens (1), (2), (3)

- New Children's Talk를 배운 학생들이 Teen Talk를 쉽게 익힐 수 있는 선행학습교재로 사용할 수 있도록 구성
- 학습의 재미와 능률을 높이기 위해 다양한 그림들과 그것들을 바탕으로 한 토론들 그리고 실제 많은 상황에서 발생하는 대화들과 수많은 지문들을 바탕으로 토론의 다양성을 확보

DISCUSSION TEXTBOOK
FROM LIS KOREA

토론교재의 베스트셀러

교사용

Debate Club for Teens (1), (2), (3) / TG

- 청소년들이 체계적으로 토론 영어를 학습할 수 있는 중·고급 교재입니다.
- 1권에서는 논리적 토론에 필요한 다양한 연습과정을 거치며, 2권에서는 제시된 다양한 주제에 대해 실전 토론을 거쳐 3권에서는 심화 주제에 대한 논리적 토론을 완성하게 됩니다.
- 청소년들의 모든 생각과 상상력을 영어로 토론할 수 있는 최상의 교재입니다.

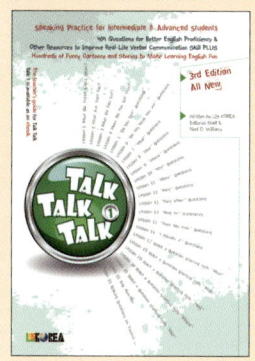

자유토론을 위한 훈련교재
3rd Edition All New
Talk Talk Talk (1)

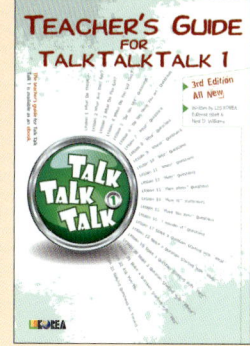

교사용
(TG)

- 새로 나온 Talk Talk Talk (1)은 전판과 비교하여, 책의 내용과 구성이 충실해졌고, 특히 각 샘플 문장마다 관련된 그림과 스토리를 더해 독자들의 흥미를 이끌어 내기 위해 많은 노력을 기울였습니다. 우리 편집진들은 400 여개의 그림과 스토리들을 통해 세상의 모든 이야기를 담으려고 했으며, 영어로 전달되는 스토리는 책 속의 또다른 재미있는 영어 학습서가 되도록 심혈을 기울였습니다. 이 책의 원래 목적인 스피킹 훈련과, 또 다른 재미있는 그림과 짧은 영어 이야기를 통해, 독자들이 한 책으로 공부와 재미 두 마리의 토끼를 잡기를 희망해 봅니다. 또한 계속해서 발행 예정인 2권, 3권에도 독자 여러분의 많은 관심 부탁드립니다.

DISCUSSION TEXTBOOK
FROM LIS KOREA

중급자들을 위한 토론교재
Speak Your Mind (1), (2)

- 일상적이며 쉬운 주제들을 선정하여 간결하게 정리했음.
- 대표 주제에 대한 질문과 대답을 여론조사 형식으로 꾸며 독자들이 쉽게 주제에 접근할 수 있도록 했음.
- 모든 주제들에 찬반 의견을 달아 독자들의 다양한 의견을 접할 수 있도록 했음.

토론교재의 베스트셀러
EXPRESS YOURSELF (1), (2), (3)
3rd Edition

- 토론 영어교재의 베스트셀러 Express Yourself 1 / 2 / 3 시리즈가 새롭게 출간되었습니다. 각 권 15개의 이슈를 깊이 있게 다루고 있으며, 다양한 토론주제와 Opinion Samples를 제공하고, 연관 dialog를 첨부하여 주제에 대한 이해력을 배가 시켰습니다.
- Points to Ponder 색션에서는 다양한 의견이 나올 수 있는 주제를 제시하여 다양한 토론이 되도록 했습니다.
- 토론주제와 연결되는 다양한 수백 개의 그림과 더불어 캡션을 덧붙여서 미국영어의 재미와 아름다움을 느끼도록 하였습니다.

DISCUSSION TEXTBOOK
FROM LIS KOREA

설명간결한 형식의 새로운 토론교재

Express Yourself Directly (1)

- Pictures Talk 섹션에서는 큰 주제에 대한 warm-up 주제들을 선정하여 그림과 함께 제시하여 본 주제에 쉽게 접근할 수 있도록 했습니다.
- Express Yourself Directly 섹션에서는 Pictures Talk 섹션에서 다루지 않은 좀 더 깊은 주제를 선정하여 심도 있는 토론이 되도록 했습니다.
- Let's Talk Funny 색션에서는 본 주제와 관련 있는 재미있는 이야기를 실어 가벼운 토론과 함께 긴장을 풀도록 했습니다.
- What Does It Mean?에서는 본 주제와 관련된 Food For Thought를 제공하여 학습자들이 자유롭게 토론 할 수 있도록 했으면 다양한 의견이 나올 수 있는 문구들을 제시하였습니다.
- 마지막으로 Synopsis에서는 (전체 400의 그림으로 구성) 각 그림에 대한 설명을 영어로 명쾌하게 제시하여 학습자가 주제에 대한 최종 복습을 할 수 있도록 했습니다.

본격적인 비지니스 토론 교재

Let's Talk Business
Major New Edition

15년 만에 새롭게 바뀐 Let's Talk Business -Major New Edition-의 특징은 다음과 같습니다.

- 현재 정보화 시대에 중요한 30개의 대표 이슈들을 선정했습니다.
- 각 이슈들은 Topic preview와 Warm-up Dialog에 의해 가볍게 다루어 지며, 또한 그림과 그림에 대한 가벼운 설명으로 독자들의 흥미를 이끌어 냅니다.
- 후에 각 이슈들은 전문적인 분석으로 상세하게 다루어지며, 이후 200개 이상의 질문으로 독자들의 의견을 이끌어 내게 됩니다.
- Current Hot Topic 섹션에서는 각 이슈에 대한 보충 이슈를 다루게 되며, 다시 한번 질문을 주어 독자들의 상상력을 자극합니다.

OPEN TO DEBATE (2): 30 Global Issues

초판 1쇄 인쇄 : 2024년 11월 01일
초판 1쇄 발행 : 2024년 11월 15일
지　은　이 : Neal D. Williams
펴　낸　곳 : (도서출판) 리스코리아
펴　낸　이 : 조은예
등　　　록 : 남양주 제 399-2011-000003호
전　　　화 : (0502) 423-7947
일러스트레이터 : 김기환
편 집 디 자 인 : 이명금, 최윤경
인　　　쇄 : 더블비

www.liskorea.com

All rights reserved. No part of this book may be reproduced, stored in a retrieval system, or transmitted in any form or by any means, electronic, mechanical, photocopying, recording or otherwise, without the prior permission in writing of the Publisher.

— Some people are scaling the fence! Aren't you going to arrest them?
— No, not at all.
— Why not? Aren't they illegal immigrants?
— Yeah, but if they succeed in scaling the fence, we'll give them citizenship. We've built the fence not because we want to block illegal immigrants but because we are testing them to see if they're strong and brave enough to scale the fence. They can join the US Army without training in boot camp. Don't you know our military forces have had difficulty recruiting new soldiers for a long time?
— How about the children? Isn't the fence too high for them to scale?
— Yes, it is. That's why we're considering lowering the fence ASAP.

The fence is too high for us! That's not fair! We thought the United States of America was a symbol of fairness in every aspect of life, including immigration. Please lower the fence at once!

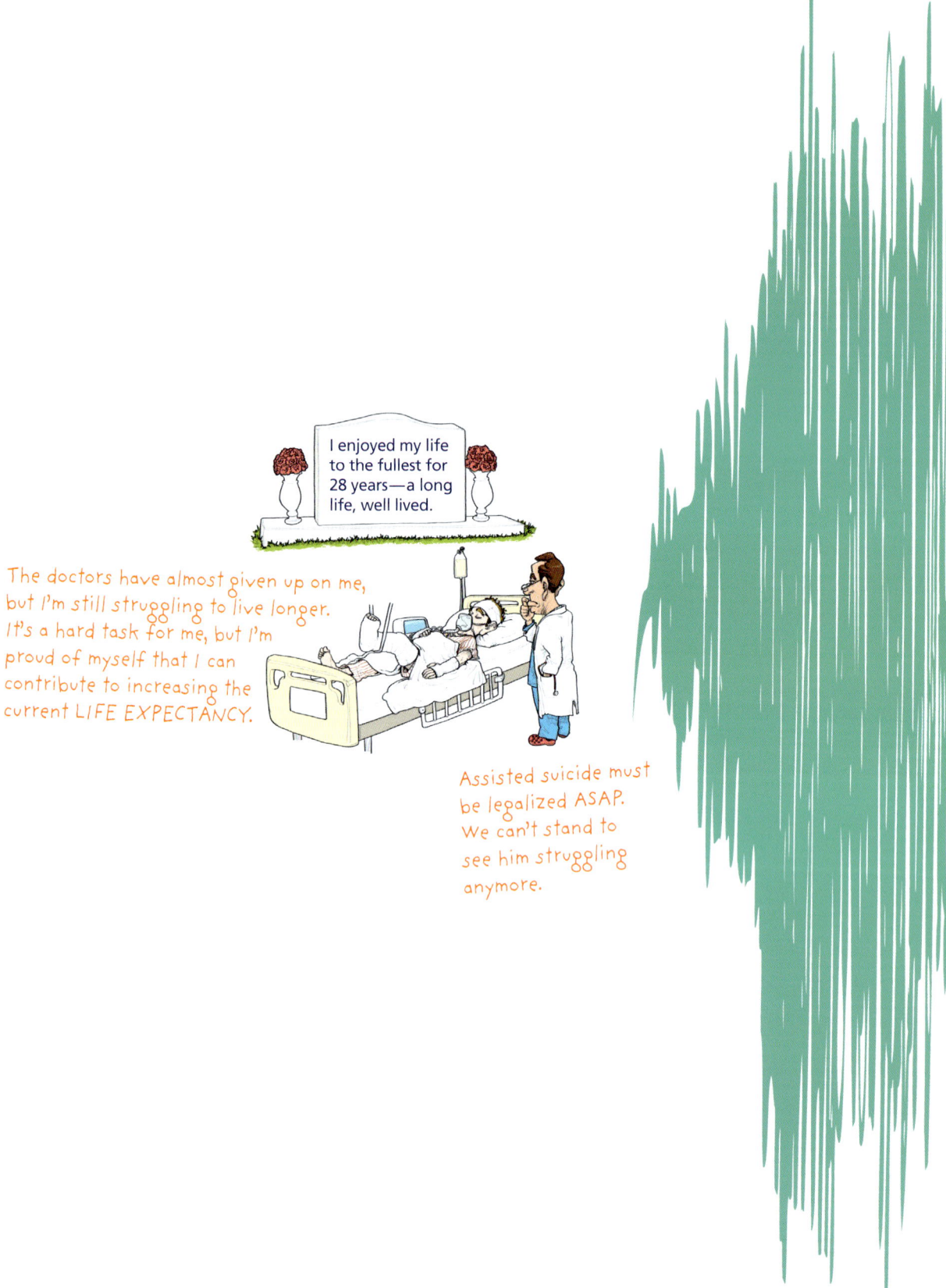

At present, we humans are facing some huge problems: we have a shortage of water, food, and energy, and at the same time, polluted water, mountains of discarded plastic, and used nuclear fuel rods pose severe dangers for us. Recently, I've won the Nobel Prize for solving these problems, all at the same time. I invented three machines. The first one purifies polluted or radioactive water, so we can drink it at once. The second one changes used plastic into noodles with the help of some chemicals, so we don't have to worry about food shortages. And the last one turns used nuclear fuel rods into firewood, so it can supply adequate and safe energy resources for us.

When I woke up in the morning, I had a horrible headache because I took a couple of sleeping pills last night. And I was so disappointed that I had a vivid, unbelievable DREAM. Anyway, I wonder if my dream will come true.

— We're arresting you.
— What for? I did nothing wrong!
— You know we have CCTVs everywhere, and we saw you buy a knife at the market.
— That's right. I'm on my way to my girlfriend's house, and we're going to make some sandwiches for lunch. It's just a bread knife.
— You're lying! We know you have a plan to murder your girlfriend after lunch.
— What? I have no idea what you're talking about!
— Don't try to fool us! We have undeniable evidence.
— What evidence? Tell me!
— Recently, we've introduced some state-of-the-art CCTVs, and they can READ YOUR MIND as well as show your movements. That's why we're arresting you for ATTEMPTED MURDER.